Francis Xavier Weninger

Catholicity, Protestantism and Infidelity

An appeal to candid Americans

Francis Xavier Weninger

Catholicity, Protestantism and Infidelity
An appeal to candid Americans

ISBN/EAN: 9783742876454

Manufactured in Europe, USA, Canada, Australia, Japa

Cover: Foto ©Lupo / pixelio.de

Manufactured and distributed by brebook publishing software (www.brebook.com)

Francis Xavier Weninger

Catholicity, Protestantism and Infidelity

CATHOLICITY,

PROTESTANTISM AND INFIDELITY.

AN APPEAL TO CANDID AMERICANS.

BY F. X. WENINGER, D. D.,
MISSIONARY OF THE SOCIETY OF JESUS.

THIRTEENTH EDITION.

NEW YORK:
SADLIER & CO., 164 WILLIAM STREET.
CINCINNATI:
JOHN P. WALSH, 170 SYCAMORE STREET,
AND FOR SALE BY ALL OTHER BOOKSELLERS IN THE U. S.
1869.

TO THE

AMERICAN PEOPLE

THESE PAGES

ARE RESPECTFULLY DEDICATED

BY THEIR SINCERE FRIEND,

THE AUTHOR.

PREFACE.

I HAVE now been in this country for upwards of twenty-two years, during which time I have labored as a Catholic missionary throughout the United States. I have traveled from place to place giving Missions, with scarcely any interruption, and have repeatedly traversed the country in every direction from Virginia to the Mexican boundaries of Texas, from New York to Minnesota. I know America, and know it far better than my own native country.

In the course of my Missions, it has often happened that Americans expressed a desire to hear me in their own language. Whenever I addressed them, I was struck with the profound attention with which they honored my extemporary efforts. I noticed on such occasions, and, indeed, in all my intercourse with the native inhabitants, so many excellent qualities of mind and heart, that I could not but view, with the sincerest feelings of compassion, so noble and intelligent a people seduced by religious error, when it would be so easy for them, by a little candid inquiry, to overcome the prejudices of education and habit, and discover that the Catholic Church is the only means of salvation for men.

Americans, I do not mean to flatter you; but I may safely assert that there is no nation upon which the Catholic Church looks with more tender solicitude than upon yours; none more worthy the labors of priests and people for their conversion.

My vocation as a Missionary among the German and the French population has seldom allowed me to address you from the pulpit. Urged on by a deep feeling of duty to aid in disabusing you of the prejudices of your Protestant education, I have thought of fulfilling this important duty of Christian and brotherly affection through the press. I hope, with the blessing of God, that my argument, if examined dispassionately and meditated on with candor, will prove amply sufficient to induce every candid man among you to acknowledge the truth of the Catholic Church.

All that is needed to test a man's sincerity, is to place before him those first principles which, like the sun in heaven, are evident by their own light. For him who closes his eyes against such evidence, whole libraries of controversial works would prove insufficient: he deliberately adheres to error, because he is unwilling to make the sacrifices which conversion to the Catholic faith would impose upon him. The mists that rise from sin exclude the sunbeams of the truth. I fear, indeed, that not a few are guilty of deliberately rejecting the well-known truth, particularly among those who find it for their worldly interests and convenience to remain Protestants.

It is not for such men these pages are written, but for that larger class who are Protestants only because they were born and brought up in Protestantism; who are sincere, willing to examine, and determined to follow their convictions. To this class it is my earnest wish that all my readers may belong.

Throughout the whole of this appeal, I mean to be plain spoken; this I owe to the importance of the subject, and to the honesty of your character; I am prompted to it by my own disposition, I am authorized in it by your example, and still more so by the plainness of the Gospel. The Gospel calls everything by its own name, and makes use of no more circumlocution in characterizing a lie, than in testifying to the truth. Disguising none of my convictions, I will tell you the truth, and even unpleasant truths expressed in the plainest language. A physician is guilty of no wrong in calling his friend's sickness by its real name, and prescribing for him the best remedies whether palatable or not: should he act otherwise, he is not a true friend. I am your friend, God knows. Never have I harbored or experienced any bitterness of feeling towards Protestants or Infidels. My only sentimen towards you, is that of love and compassion; my only wish, to extend to you a brother's hand, and to help to save you. Your salvation is my only object in offering you these pages; and I have no doubt that, before laying down the book, you will be fully convinced of it.

My arguments, I hope, will be solid; but in order to give to the work the character of a friendly conversation, rather than of a dry polemical discussion, I shall occasionally introduce some incidents of my missionary life. While such incidents will serve to illustrate my proofs, they will, perhaps, also enable you to read the work with less fatigue and more interest.

Americans, read, reflect, and decide for yourselves.

THE AUTHOR.

TABLE OF CONTENTS.

	PAGE
Preface	v
Introduction	1

CHAPTER I.

The Character of Protestantism 5

SECTION I.

CONTROVERTED DOGMAS COMPARED.

The Primitive Condition of Man and the Fall	7
The Redemption	13
The Church	17
The Means of Salvation	31
Baptism	34
Confirmation	35
The Eucharist	37
Penance—Indulgences	49

	PAGE
Extreme Unction	58
Holy Orders	62
Matrimony	66
Good Works	68
Purgatory	72
The Communion of Saints	76

SECTION II.

Consequences	85
Ulterior Consequences	88

CHAPTER II.

| The Principle of Protestantism | 104 |

SECTION I.

Strength of the Catholic Principle, which is, that the Teaching of the True Church of Christ is the true Rule of Faith	104
Unanswerable Proof, founded on the mark of Apostolicity, that the Catholic Church is the true Church of Christ	106
The Other Marks of the True Church of Christ belong only to the Catholic Church	122
Unity	124
Holiness	131
Universality	139
Indestructibility	143

CONCLUSIVE PROOF OF THE INFALLIBILITY OF THE CATHOLIC CHURCH, AS THE TRUE CHURCH OF CHRIST—HER INFALLIBILITY IS THE RULE OF FAITH 153

SECTION II.

THE WEAKNESS AND ABSURDITY OF THE PROTESTANT RULE OF FAITH.. 163
THE PRIVATE INTERPRETATION OF THE BIBLE HAS NONE OF THE REQUISITES OF A TRUE RULE OF FAITH 165
The Rule of Faith must be—
Clear 166
Complete 169
As old as the Faith itself 171
Universal 173
Accessible to every one, and Final 174
THE PROTESTANT RULE OF FAITH LACKS ALL THESE CHARACTERISTICS—THE CATHOLIC RULE OF FAITH POSSESSES THEM ALL 177

CHAPTER III.

PROTESTANT PREJUDICES 181

SECTION I.

RELIGIOUS PREJUDICES 191
The Pope 191
The Clergy 194
Confession 198
Indulgences 203
The Bible 204
Saints 206

	PAGE
Mary	213
Celibacy	216
Holy Mass	220
Communion	221
Use of the Latin Language	222
Ceremonies	226
Abstinence	229
Exclusive Salvation	230

SECTION II.

POLITICAL PREJUDICES	234
Allegiance	244
The Inquisition	244
Despotism	249
Civilization	250
Morality	254
The Sabbath	256
The Sovereignty of the Pope and his Civil Government	257
Republicanism	261
Freedom of Discussion	265

CHAPTER IV.

INFIDELITY THE ULTIMATE CONSEQUENCE OF PROTESTANTISM	278

SECTION I.

INFIDELITY REFUTED.——SEVEN CONCLUSIVE ARGUMENTS AGAINST INFIDELITY	280
The Undeniable Existence of God	280
The Undeniable Immortality of the Soul	283

	PAGE
The Undeniable Necessity of Religion	287
The Undeniable Necessity of a Divinely Revealed Religion	288
The Undeniably Divine Mission of Christ	291
The Undeniable Superhuman Character of the Church of Christ	304
The Undeniable Axiom "Where Peter is, there is the Church"	306

SECTION II.

OBJECTIONS ANSWERED	309
The Incomprehensibility of Mysteries	309
Everlasting Punishment,	315
The Supposed Contradiction of Revelation with Geology and History,	327
CONCLUSION,	333

INTRODUCTION.

When we examine into the real character of Protestantism, taking into consideration its starting point, and its logical tendency, we are forced to pass upon it a judgment, which may seem harsh and offensive, but which is nevertheless legitimately true. This judgment regards more especially the psychological characteristic of Protestantism, to which, perhaps, sufficient attention has not been hitherto called. It is the startling fact, that Protestantism, as taught by the early Reformers and as held in substance to the present day, has rejected precisely those articles of the Catholic Creed, which are best calculated to inspire consolation and hope, and has set up, instead, just such doctrines as must inevitably sadden and crush the soul, and ultimately lead to utter despair.

That characteristic if true, is, you will acknowledge, fatal to the claims of Protestantism considered as a Divine Religion. It is so evidently incompatible with the wants of the heart and the requirements of reason, that on the supposition of Catholicity and Protestantism being both of them mere human inventions, it would be easier to explain how Protestants could have become Catholics, than to assign a valid reason why Catholics should ever have become Protestants; for who would not choose to believe doctrines tending to cheer and console, rather than such as are only fit to crush the heart and lead a man to despair? I consider it one of the most astonishing facts in all history, that your ancestors rejected Catholicity with all its consolations, and adopted, instead, a Religion of distress and despair. Such a choice could never have been the effect of calm reflection, but must have been, as history proves it was, the result of violence and blind passion.

To prove my assertion it is not necessary to demonstrate the divinity of the Catholic Church and her doctrines; I shall do that, in a brief and conclusive manner, in a subsequent part of the work, when I come to the discussion of the principle of faith. Neither is it necessary that my Protestant readers should in all respects agree with the early Reformers. To establish the point at issue. it is enough to show that the early Reformers held the doctrines of distress and despair which I ascribe to them, and that the doctrines of Protestantism at the present day are still the same in substance in many respects, and in principle the same in every respect.

I do not undertake to write a long and tedious polemical discussion, nor a symbolic like Mœhler's or Buchmann's; I simply intend to make a comparison between the doctrines of Protestants and Catholics, and to examine them in their nature and logical consequences.

I feel confident that at every step in the comparison you will find a convincing proof of my charges against Protestantism; and the Catholic doctrine will appear to you not only consoling, but so much in harmony with all the wants of man, that it could only have proceeded from a Divine hand, bearing upon its face the evident seal of divine truth and beauty. I have as little doubt that you will discover, that Protestantism, by its rejection of Catholic doctrine has disfigured the beauty of the Christian Creed, and robbed you of the sweetest and holiest consolations of life, along with your only hope of eternal salvation.

Having reviewed the principal points controverted between Catholics and Protestants, I shall be justified in asking you with astonishment, How could your forefathers have accepted so extraordinary a Religion? and how can their descendants cling to a religious system so void of hope and consolation?

In the next place, I will show you, that the only obstacles to your return to the Catholic Church, are a lack of earnest examination into the principle of faith, and your adherence to unfounded anti-Catholic prejudices.

Finally, I shall briefly, yet unanswerably, refute Infidelity, the last logical consequence of Protestantism.

Accordingly the work is divided into four chapters, treating successively of the Character of Protestantism, of the Principle of Protestantism, of the Prejudices of Protestants, and of the last logical consequence of Protestantism, Infidelity.

CHAPTER I.

THE CHARACTER OF PROTESTANTISM.

By the character of Protestantism I understand that peculiar mark which stamps the whole Protestant system as a Religion of distress and despair. To prove that such is its real character, I shall review its doctrines as compared with those of the Catholic Church. In doing so, to be as brief and plain as possible, I will follow a chronological order, and compare in succession the Catholic doctrine with the opposite Protestant view, on the condition of our First Parents, the Fall, the Redemption, the Church, and the Means of Salvation given us by our Redeemer. Whatever I advance on these topics, in regard to Protestantism, I shall support by quotations from the writings and approved Formularies of Faith of the early Reformers, or by referring to public facts and professions with which every well-informed man is acquainted.

SECTION I.

CONTROVERTED DOGMAS COMPARED.

THE FIRST CONDITION, AND THE FALL OF MAN.

In the condition of our first parents, the Catholic doctrine distinguishes, in particular, two things, nature and grace, or the nature of our first parents, and their supernatural state. This doctrine is illustrated by the Fathers of the Church from the text of Genesis, " God created man after His own image and likeness " By the image here spoken of, they understand the reason and free-will of man ; and by the likeness, his state of union with God by supernatural grace. The Catholic Church teaches, that by their supernatural state of union with God, our first parents became children of God and heirs of heaven. If they remained obedient to God, they were to be exempt from death, and, at the close of their trial on earth, to be admitted to the Beatific Vision, a state of higher supernatural union with God in heaven. They were destined to see God face to face, to be transfigured in Him, entering into His glory and His bliss, in beatific union with the blessed spirits for all eternity. There is not a heart on earth but must feel the beauty, the sublimity, the bliss of the condition of our first parents, as taught by the Catholic Church.

In the next place, the Catholic Church teaches, that our first parents were free to remain in their blessed condition, or to forfeit it, that is, free to sin or not to sin.

Lastly, the Catholic Church teaches, that by the fall, man lost the likeness only of God, that is, his state of supernatural grace; but that the image of God, that is, his natural reason and free-will were only impaired, not destroyed. Hence, according to the Catholic doctrine, man, after the fall, retained the ability to perform good actions, in the natural order, and remained free as he was before the fall.

This doctrine surely is most consoling, for there is a comfort even in our losses, when we feel that something yet remains, and we can look forward to the time when, with what remains, our losses may still be repaired.

Protestantism refuses you this comfort. In

its original teaching and logical tendency, it denies the Catholic doctrine of the first condition of man, as well as the Catholic doctrine of the fall. It denies the possibility of man's real restoration, and takes a most distressing view of his condition. Here are my proofs. In regard to the original condition of man, Luther, and Calvin, and their early adherents taught, that our first parents were not raised to a supernatural state, but, with all their high gifts, were left in a purely natural condition. With regard to the fall, they taught the doctrine of total depravity. According to their doctrine, the image of God was destroyed in man by the disobedience of our first parents; man's freewill was by it lost forever, and man has retained only the power of sinning; so that no good human action, even in the natural order, is possible in our present state, and what men deem their virtues, are merely so many sins and splendid abominations before God. Quenstedt, a Lutheran theologian of the seventeenth century, collected the opinions of Luther on this subject from the Reformer's own works. Luther's doctrine, in his own words, is as follows: " To sin was man's nature after his fall." 'Man himself is nothing but sin." "What is born of a father and mother, is nothing but sin."* It is well known that Luther wrote a whole work, entitled "*De Servo Arbitrio*"—"*On Slave-Will*," in which he labors to prove, that by the fall, man lost his free-will, so as to have become incapable of choosing deliberately between good and evil ; and that whatever he does, he does by an irresistible impulse, either good or evil, according as God or Satan overpowers his will. The original and elegant comparison he makes use of to illustrate his point, is generally known : he compares the will of man, after the fall, to—an ass. " If God rides him," says Luther, " He drives him whithersoever He will, to do good : if the devil rides him, he drives him as he wishes." " Whatever happens, happens necessarily, though to us it may appear to be done freely." This assertion Luther repeats again and again in the work just quoted. In another work, he says, " Free-will does nothing, because there is no free-will."†

What is still more shocking, is that Luther views this state of total depravity with delight. He says, " Even if man could have free-will, he would not like it, for it would only disquiet

---

* Quenstedt, Theolog. Didact. Polem. part. II. Wittenberg, 1669. Cf. Bellarm., De Statu Protop.; and Luther, com. 3. in Gen.

† Luther. Adv. Erasm. Rotterdam.

him. But as it is, I can say and believe, I commit evil, but God does not punish me, because I believe. So I feel quiet."*

Thus Protestantism, as taught by the first Reformer, plucks up by the root the highest blessing of our lives, our consciousness of freedom.

Melanchthon, the faithful interpreter of the doctrines of Luther his master, calls the dogma of free-will " a slanderous doctrine, which has gradually insinuated itself into Christianity, and originated with the heathens." "Man," he says, " can of himself do nothing but commit sin, just as fire burns, and the magnet attracts iron. To assert the contrary, is to be a Pelagian."†

Calvin repeats the same doctrine: " Everything in man, after his fall, is sin. The virtues of the heathens, such as those of Socrates, Xenocrates, and Zeno, were only splendid crimes."‡

If all this is true, the fall, though we had no personal share in it, must have changed us into incarnate demons. Such, at the very outset, is the conclusion to which Protestantism logically

---

* De Servo Arbit. f. 236.
† Melanchth. Loc. Theol., pp. 19, 122.
‡ Calv. Inst. l. ii. c. 1 et 3.

leads; one which alone would be sufficient to overwhelm us with distress.

The worst of it is, that this doctrine is not peculiar to the chiefs of the Reformation, but has passed into the principles of Protestantism as appears from the Formularies of Faith and the symbolical writings of the early Protestants. They do not all, in express terms, go so far as Luther, Melanchthon, Calvin, or Zwingli, but they proceed far enough to imply the whole doctrine by logical sequence. The most important among the early Protestant symbolical writings, is the Formula of Concord, or "*Solida Declaratio*" of the year 1577. That Formula says expressly, " The likeness of God has disappeared in consequence of original sin, and an evil substance has penetrated into the spiritual being of man, whereby that being has become most abominable."[*] The Swiss, Belgian, and Scottish Confessions of Faith, contain, in substance, the very same doctrine.

In opposition to this doctrine the Council of Trent enacted the following canon: " If any one shall say, that all the works which are done before justification, in whatever manner they may be done, are really sins, or deserve the

---

[*] Solid. Declar. c. 9 and 10. De Peccat. Orig. § 2 and 22. II. De Lib. Arbit. § 14.

hatred of God ; or, that the more a man strives to dispose himself for grace, the more grievously he sins ; let him be anathema."*

Calvin, Zwingli, and their adherents even go so far as to assert that Adam could not help falling, because God had decreed that he should fall.†

Americans, are you ready to admit doctrines like these, inculcating, as they do, the most blasphemous libel on the justice and sanctity of God, and the principle best calculated to banish all consolation from the soul ; leaving man to groan helplessly under the weight of irremediable wickedness, and under the irresistible tyranny of an unjust God ? ? ? ? ?

THE REDEMPTION.

In misfortune we long for relief. When relief is given, we are consoled ; when loss is changed into gain, and good drawn out of evil, our consolation rises in proportion to our former sorrow. This, if we accept the Catholic doctrine, is an image of the nature and the effects of the Redemption.

* Conc. Trid. Sess. VI. can. VII.
† Calvin. Instit. l. i., cap. 18, § 2. ; l. iii., c, 23, § 8 and 4 Bezn, Adv. Calum Genev. 1861. Zwinglius, De Provid. 5 and 6.

The Church teaches, that, to redeem us from original sin and its consequences, Christ the Son of God assumed our nature and died for us on the Cross; that, by His merits, we are really freed from sin, and by the infusion of supernatural sanctifying grace into our souls, are again united to God, and become personally pleasing in His sight. You will not deny, that it is an immense consolation for man, after having been tortured by remorse, and weighed down by the sense of unworthiness, to know that he has been really pardoned, that he is once more really free from guilt, truly pure and holy before His Maker.

The Catholic Church further teaches, that man co-operates in his justification by co-operating, with perfect freedom, with the grace of God, which prompts and strengthens him to do penance and amend his life. To be allowed to co-operate with the grace of God, renders his consolation still greater, for it makes him conscious of a meritorious personal triumph over his own passions and over the power of Satan.

Indeed, in the Redemption we have gained far more, infinitely more, I might almost say, than we lost in Adam: hence, the triumphal chant of the Catholic Church in the solemn service on Holy Saturday, " O happy fault, which has deserved so great and glorious a Redeemer." For our Saviour has not only conquered Satan, and released us from his power; He has not only raised us to a supernatural state of grace, like that in which Adam was constituted; but He has, besides, enabled us to practice higher virtues than Adam could have practiced in the state of unfallen nature, and prepared for us a proportionately higher glory in heaven. By the union of the Divine with the human nature He has raised our nature above the angelic choirs, and communicated to us a grace far more powerful and of much higher dignity than was originally imparted to our first parents. A far higher field of virtue is opened before us in the accomplishment of the Christian law, and the keeping of the evangelical counsels. According to the Catholic doctrine, the natural consequences of the fall, concupiscence and the sufferings of life, may be turned by us, if we will, into occasions of new and most glorious merits and proportionate reward in eternity, so that our condition, after the fall, may even, in some respect, be envied by the angels, who could never, by sufferings, prove their obedience and their love of God. Thus the Catholic doctrine allows us to taste the full sweetness of the Redemption, to enjoy its efficacy, and have a real share with our

Saviour in His triumphant resurrection from the dead and complete victory over the powers of darkness.

Of this consolation Protestantism deprives you. The doctrine of Luther, Calvin, and their adherents, is, that no sin, whether original or personal, is ever remitted; but is, at best, only *covered* by the merits of Christ.* According to their doctrine, man, after being justified through Christ, remains in sin as much as before, with this only difference, that, after his justification, he is not liable to be punished for his sins. For a man who loves his God it is hard to conceive a more distressing doctrine: to such a man the offence is more hateful than the punishment, and he finds the thought intolerable, that God, though unwilling to punish him, yet should allow him to be no better in His sight than a whitened sepulchre. Besides, it is a genuine Protestant doctrine, that man has no share whatsoever in thus covering his sins, because he has altogether lost his freewill, and is as passive in the act of his justification, to use one of Luther's illustrations, as the pillar of salt into which the wife of Lot was changed.† After his justification, as before it,

---

* Luther. Expos. Epist. ad Galat. Solid. Declar. III. § 15. Calvin. Instit. l. III. c. ii.

† Luther, in Genes. cap. xix.

man remains completely incapable of performing any really good work, or of gaining any real merit before God.

Thus Protestantism would leave no true state of justice on earth ; it would banish the heavenly consciousness of innocence regained ;. it would make us believe, if possible, that the wounds inflicted by the fall are so deep, that the blood of the Redeemer cannot heal them; our ruin so hopeless that the mercy of the Almighty cannot repair it. Such is the second stage of its distressing system. Do you think it preferable to the Catholic view ?

THE CHURCH.

In all our undertakings, and especially when great interests are at stake, we wish for security. In the pursuit of knowledge, we long for *certainty*. When some important object is to be attained, we are glad to find that the way to attain it, is obvious and free from danger, or, if uncertain, that we have some faithful friend to guide us.

When there is question, not merely of a temporal object, but of eternal life, it is of infinitely more importance to us to know with certainty the way that leads to it, and that the way should be secure. No questions can be imagined of greater importance for us, than these: Am I, or am I not, in the way that leads to salvation? Am I, or am I not, in the true Religion? Is my faith infallibly certain, or is it not? Is there any answer to be found on earth, that can satisfy my mind on these all-important questions? Protestants and Catholics agree that the answer is to be sought for in the true faith. But here another question arises. Is there any *authority* on earth, that can fully clear up all doubts, and give unerring certainty, on these momentous questions?

The Catholic answers in the affirmative. The Catholic doctrine is, that Christ has instituted an *infallible* Church, to whose guardianship He has intrusted His doctrines and the means of salvation, and which He established forever. That Church is the Catholic Church. As the infallible guardian of the Word of God, whether written or unwritten, she teaches whatever Christ has taught her; as His infallible representative, she ministers to men all the means of salvation which He has given her. The Catholic doctrine furthermore asserts, that the mission of the Catholic Church, as the infallible teacher and unerring guide of men, will remain unaltered to the end of time. Through her Christ unites the earth to heaven; and that union, like her mission, will last as long as the world. " Behold, I am with you all days, even to the consummation of the world."*

In the Church we have a guide to whom we can intrust our salvation with the same security as to Christ Himself. " He that heareth you, heareth me."† " And I say to thee, That thou art Peter, and upon this rock I will build my church, and the gates of hell shall not prevail against it. And I will give to thee the keys of the kingdom of heaven; and whatsoever thou shalt bind on earth, it shall be bound also in heaven: and whatsoever thou shalt loose on earth, it shall be loosed also in heaven."‡

Trusting to the guidance of the Catholic Church, the lowest and the most ignorant among the faithful, is as secure of his faith, as certain of the way of salvation, as the highest and the most learned. Through his own special pastor, placed over him by his bishop, every Catholic is in communion with his bishop, and, through the bishop, in communion with the legitimate successor of St. Peter, on whom

* Matt., xxviii. 20.
† Luke, x. 16.
‡ Matt., xvi. 18, 19.

Christ Himself conferred the care and guidance of His whole flock: "Feed my lambs, feed my sheep."* " I have prayed for thee, that thy faith fail not: and thou being once converted, confirm thy brethren."† United to the successor of St. Peter, every one of us has the right to appeal confidently to the celebrated canon of St. Ambrose, " *Ubi Petrus, ibi Ecclesia —Where Peter is, there is the Church.*"

The whole history of the Catholic Church, confirms the Catholic in his faith, and in the consolation that he is unmistakably in the way of salvation. We look back through eighteen centuries, all bearing witness to the truth of our faith. At the very birth of the Catholic Church, and in the first three centuries of her existence, we have seventeen millions of martyrs, our elder brethren in the faith, all sealing with their blood the very same Catholic faith that we profess to-day. The testimony of the first three centuries is continued through all centuries: in all ages, the divinity of the Catholic faith has been testified by the blood of true martyrs, all children of the Catholic Church. In our own days, the plains and cities of Corea, China, Tonquin, Cochin-China, Syria,

* John, xxi. 15, 17.
† Luke, xxii, 32.

reddened with the blood of martys, have renewed to the world the testimony given to all past generations.

We look back through eighteen hundred years of triumph. The Catholic Church has not only survived all persecutions; she has found powerful and bitter enemies in her own bosom, and has survived them all. Heresy, leagued with the power of kings and emperors, has not ceased to wage against her a more deadly war than even the early persecutors. The Catholic Church still stands, where she was placed by the Hand of the Almighty, calm upon the rock of ages, upheld by the promises of eternity, the waves ever raging madly against her, and forever breaking at her feet. Everything has changed around her; her faith and her spiritual power remain unchanged.

The testimony of hosts of martyrs, extending through all ages, the perpetuity of the Catholic Church in spite of all attacks, would be amply sufficient to authorize the faith of the Catholic, even had he no other proof; but another host of witnesses, the Saints of the Catholic Church, a countless number of Catholics, men and women distinguished and admired for their heroic virtues, give him an additional security that his faith is Divine. The annals of the

Catholic Church, and the annals of the world, have recorded the long roll of her apostolic men, whose voice has carried the glad tidings of salvation to every nation on the globe. Upon every page of the history of the Church and of the world for eighteen centuries, the Catholic finds recorded the names of men and women, illustrious for their beneficence, and whose unobtrusive greatness of virtue has attracted the veneration of the world. Along the whole line of by-gone Christian ages, the Catholic meets with a genealogy of men, doctors, bishops, popes, eminent for talent, genius, power, virtue, holiness, such as no other society can exhibit. Rome, in particular, from St. Peter down to Pius IX., has been illustrated by a succession of pontiffs, whose virtues, zeal, and heroism, shine through her history like the stars in the firmament, and mark her triumphal progress through her exile in time to her home in eternity.

To sum up, as a Catholic I am infallibly certain that my faith is true, because the Catholic Church is infallible; I am infallibly certain that I am in the way of salvation, because the Catholic Church that guides me, cannot err. My faith is confirmed by the testimony of millions of martyrs; the guidance in which I trust has led millions of the most illustrious of our race to heaven. They all followed the same path of faith which I follow, and walking in their footsteps, I can not doubt, that the path is a safe one, the true path that leads to heaven. This is my consolation, great in proportion to the eternal objects which we pursue.

Of this consolation Protestantism utterly deprives you. In your Protestant view, the Church is only an aggregate of many separate members. Every Protestant explicitly holds, that there is no infallible Church: he regards the claim of infallibility in matters of faith as an insult to God, accuses the first Church of apostasy, and brands her with the name of Antichrist.

In your opinion, Christ has instituted no infallible ecclesiastical authority. The fundamental doctrine of Protestantism is, that God has ordered all men to search the Bible, and to make out of it a faith, each for himself, in the best way he can; that the private interpretation of the Bible replaces, and ought by right to replace the authority of the Church, and must be held as the only Rule of Faith.

This is a distressing doctrine, for it makes it absolutely impossible to arrive at any certainty in matters of faith. As I shall show more fully afterwards, you cannot even prove that the

Bible is the Bible, or is an inspired book, unless you abandon your Rule of Faith, and appeal to the authority of the Catholic Church. Unless you assume the infallibility of the Church, who has given you the Bible, and defined that it is the word of God, I confidently challenge you to produce a single proof of the inspiration of the whole Bible, such as will satisfy even your own mind. In the whole Scripture, you cannot show a single passage, in which it is revealed that the *whole* Bible is inspired; and, while you admit the Bible alone as your Rule of Faith, and reject Tradition and the authority of the Catholic Church, you will look in vain elsewhere for your proof. But even granting, for the sake of argument, that you have proved the inspiration of the whole Bible to the satisfaction of intelligent men, whence do you derive any infallible certainty that you understand it, and that you do not err essentially in the faith which you extract from it?

Here lies the great difference between the consoling security of the Catholic, and the distressing *insecurity* of the Protestant. The Catholic relies on the *infallibility* of the Church, and hence is infallibly sure that his faith is Divine. The Protestant, as such, having nothing beyond his private interpretation to rely on, cannot attain to any thing higher than a mere private *opinion* very liable to error. The Catholic rests on the infallible promise of Christ, that " the gates of hell shall not prevail against the Church." The Protestant has to meet and cannot get rid of the fearful denunciation of Christ, " If he will not hear the Church, let him be to thee as the heathen, and the publican."* The Catholic sails securely in the imperishable bark of Peter. The Protestant clings to a wretched plank, thrown out upon a raging sea : perhaps he may be saved by it : this is the utmost limit of his hope. The Catholic Church can confidently say to her children, " Trust to my guidance, I am of God. Let your lives correspond to your faith, and you will be saved." Protestantism, throwing into the hands of its adherents a venerable book dishonored by a thousand conflicting interpretations, says to them, " Read for yourselves, and discover the truth, if you can ; make out your own faith, and hold fast to it, if you are able ; perhaps it will save you." Can the human heart be placed in a more distressing condition ? At best, you can only say, " It may be that I have succeeded in discovering the truth ; but it may also be that I have failed,

* John, xxvi. 17.

and, if so, what is to become of my soul in eternity?"

Some fanatic Protestant religionists, to escape the uncertainty inevitably attending all purely human opinions, have set up the doctrine of Private *Inspiration;* they affect to believe in an inward teaching of the Holy Spirit, and would fain persuade themselves, that this imaginary guidance is as safe as the infallible authority of a Divinely commissioned Church. This pretended inspiration they themselves ultimately resolve into mere feeling, which, of all sources of error, is the most open to alarming illusions. Indeed, it is hard to conceive how any man of common intelligence can be so rash as to build his faith, and his hope of heaven on so delusive a foundation. All the world knows to what extravagance some Protestant sects, especially the Methodist,*

* I here wish to direct your attention again to what I have already remarked in the Preface. I only censure errors in doctrine, not persons. It is my firm conviction that in the ranks of the Methodists, especially American Methodists, there are, as well as in other sects, large numbers of honest and very respectable persons. They only indulge in excitements like those referred to in the text, because they feel an immense want of some signs of certainty about their salvation; and being uninstructed in the Catholic doctrine, they give way to such delusions. If, in the course of the discussion, I mention the Methodists more

allow themselves to be carried, in consequence of the principle of Private Inspiration. The excitement, on some occasions, amounts to real religious intoxication. I hope the expression will not offend any one. I appeal to the impression which must occasionally have been made on every one of my readers, on passing by a Methodist camp meeting, and hearing the discordant singing, the howling, and screaming, and witnessing the jumping and contortions, in which those inspired religionists indulge. Every sober-minded man must feel, that such disgraceful exhibitions have, by no means, the sign of a Divine influence. The religious intoxication vanishes; fanaticism gives way to sober thoughts; doubts return with fresh vigor upon the poor victim of delusion; his faith, that delighted him yesterday, appears to him uncertain, and racks his mind to-day.

Now Methodism is but one of the countless sects that have been disputing, for three centuries, about the meaning of the Bible, and

---

frequently than other Protestants, it is not because I have a less friendly feeling towards them, but because they are the most numerous and active Protestant denomination in this country.

have pretty nearly exhausted all imaginable extravagances and all possible contradictions.

Such is the result at which you have arrived. You have set up the principle of Private Interpretation as your only Rule of Faith. The legitimate consequence has been your conflicting sects, and as many conflicting opinions as there are independent minds in Protestantism. The aspect of so much discord, so much confusion, so much uncertainty, can surely present no comfort to the human soul, born for the truth, and invincibly desirous of possessing it in security. It is clear that a religious system which unavoidably leads to such results, necessarily engendering in its own bosom an endless multiplicity of contradictory systems, cannot have come from God, and, therefore, cannot be true. God is Truth: the Spirit of Truth cannot reveal contradictions. Truth, like God, is one and unchangeable: a faith, therefore, that comes from God, must be one, like Him, and cannot change. Your faith has changed, and is ever changing. It cannot, therefore, be true. Luther himself shuddered at the sight of the vast variety of inconsistent tenets that had sprung out of his principle, even in his own day, and, at times, could not help confessing that he saw in them an evident mark of error and falsehood. To-day the state of things is worse than ever. Where, at the present time, is the Protestantism of Luther and the early Reformers? I question whether a single Protestant can now be found, who holds the same doctrines with them in all respects. Protestantism bears upon its face, more clearly marked than ever, the unmistakable seal of error.

Here, then, my Protestant friends, you have, on one side, the sublime attitude of the Catholic Church, claiming to be Divinely commissioned and Divinely guided, her faith infallible and unchangeable, her chief on earth representing her unity and maintaining it; a Church, whose unerring guidance gives absolute security in the way of salvation. On the other side, you have the fluctuating conduct of your sects, endless changes of opinion which no logic can reconcile, interminable disputes, confessions of faith framed to-day, and obsolete to-morrow, teachers opposed to teachers, leaders without authority or influence, except that founded on momentary fashion or caprice; and hence no possible security in the way of salvation.

With or without the Bible, learned or unlearned, the Catholic is secure. Protestantism leaves the ignorant without resource, and the learned without certainty; the ignorant cannot avail themselves of the principle of private interpretation, and the learned avai themselves of it in vain. To pretend to give even a tolerable interpretation of the Bible, learning is required: the highest learning, left to its own private interpretations, has not succeeded, never can succeed, in framing a reliable system of faith, whilst the claim of Private Inspiration set forth by some of the Protestant sects, is but a vain and desperate effort to possess Infallibility by infatuation rather than by authority.

The contrast between Catholicity and Protestantism, in regard to the teaching authority, needs no further comment. In point of company, Protestantism is equally unsatisfactory. The Catholic treads in the footsteps of millions of men illustrious for virtue, of whose salvation there can be no doubt. Can you point to a parallel series of Protestant martyrs, confessors, doctors, fathers, virgins, benefactors of mankind, all unquestionably eminent for heroic Christian virtue, and of whose salvation you can entertain no doubt? If you can, please let us have a list of their names. Even if you claimed any Protestant saints, would you be able to show that they held the very same faith with you? This you have no means of determining for there is neither a common Protestant infallible authority to which all submit, nor a common Protestant standard of faith to which all conform. The Catholic is sure that every Catholic saint believed as he does, neither more nor less, because every Catholic believes what the Church teaches as of faith, neither more nor less. You cannot know of a single one of your great men, whether he held the same faith with you or not.

Luther evidently made a dangerous experiment, to say the least, when he left the highway by which millions, for fifteen centuries, under the infallible guidance of the Church, had gone to heaven, and chose to grope in a by-way, with his private notions for his only guide, and no means of determining whether his course led to heaven or to perdition. Time has only made the experiment more alarming.

THE MEANS OF SALVATION.

When a great object is to be attained, it is not enough to know how to attain it: we must also have the means. It would be of little use to know the way of salvation, if we had no effectual means of saving our souls. In the way of salvation we have many wants, which the grace of God alone can supply.

In the Catholic Church every want of the soul is amply provided for. The Catholic doctrine on this subject is, that for every general want Christ has instituted in His Church a particular means of grace. These means are the Sacraments. Of the consolations to be derived from them none but a practical Catholic can form any adequate idea.

It is the doctrine of the Catholic Church, that Christ instituted seven Sacraments, each of them corresponding to a great general necessity, and all of them together answering all the spiritual wants of the soul. As the supernatural life bears an analogy to the natural, so the means of grace have an analogy to natural necessities. In the natural order, man is born, has need of strength and nourishment, and of medicine in sickness; in the supernatural order, he is spiritually born by Baptism, strengthened by Confirmation, nourished by the Holy Eucharist, restored to spiritual health by the sacrament of Penance. Besides, as there are two principal conditions of Christian life, each with peculiar and important duties, and consequently with grave and peculiar wants, the Clerical state and that of Wedlock, there are two other sacraments, Holy Orders and Matrimony, the latter sanctifying marriage and giving grace to fulfil its duties, the former conferring Ecclesiastical power with grace to use it worthily. Lastly, for the hour of death, when man stands in greater need than ever of spiritual strength and consolation, and his fate for eternity is to be decided by his last actions, Christ, according to the Catholic doctrine, instituted the Sacrament of Extreme Unction.

Of these seven sources of grace, Protestantism has kept only two, or rather none. Protestants, indeed, generally hold Baptism to be a Sacrament, though many among them look upon it as a mere rite conferring no grace. But whether you admit it as a Sacrament or not, the Sacrament of Baptism does not properly belong to Protestantism, for, as I shall show a little further on, there is only one true Church, viz., the Catholic Church, the gate of which is Baptism, and so every one truly baptized, becomes a member, not of a Protestant sect, but of the Catholic Church. With regard to the Holy Eucharist, Protestants have retained it only in name, for rejecting Holy Orders, they have no true Bishops, and therefore no true Priests, clothed with the power of changing bread and wine into the Body and Blood of Christ.

But allowing, for the sake of argument, that you have the Sacraments of Baptism and the Holy Eucharist, in substance as well as in name, still it remains true, that the Protestant doctrine deprives you of the consolations of these and all the other Sacraments of the Catholic Church. This I will show at some length.

THE SACRAMENTS.

I. BAPTISM.

The Catholic Church teaches that Baptism really remits sin, and washes away every stain of sin; that man, "born again of water and the Holy Ghost," is raised by it to a state of supernatural grace, and enters the glorious condition of the children of God, becoming in a peculiar manner entitled to call God his Father, and vested, as the heir and brother of Christ, with a right to heaven. At the moment of Baptism, he is associated with the angels, as a future citizen of heaven. By the sanctification of baptismal grace, he is rendered capable of meriting before God, of increasing his merits daily and hourly throughout the whole course of his life, and by the increase of his merits, heightening the crown won for him by the blood of his Redeemer. This very consoling doctrine must, I think, come home to every heart.

Of this Protestantism deprives you, for it acknowledges no real remission of sin by Baptism, but at best only a covering of sin by the merits of Christ, and rejects personal merit, with every thing else that follows from the Catholic doctrine. Many sects look on Baptism as a mere ceremony, conferring no grace, right, or effect whatsoever. Hence, it is no wonder that many Protestants have come to regard Baptism with complete indifference. It is no wonder that there are large numbers in Protestant countries who do not care to be baptized at all, or who are baptized late in life, and then either invalidly through some essential defect in the administration, or unworthily through the lack of the necessary disposition on their part. This is especially the case in America. Millions of men in this country, calling themselves Christians, and members of the various Protestant denominations, have never been baptized. Protestantism is ending in the desolation of heathenism.

II. CONFIRMATION.

A true Christian wishes to lead a life worthy

of his faith, and earnestly desires the strength necessary to do so.

The Catholic Church teaches that the Sacrament of Confirmation confers the strength which he needs. Whoever receives that sacrament worthily becomes a living temple of the Holy Ghost, a well-armed champion in the cause of Christ. If he remains faithful in co-operating with the grace which he has received, the Holy Ghost will continue to dwell in him, " the Spirit of wisdom and of understanding, the Spirit of counsel and of fortitude, the Spirit of knowledge and of godliness, and the Spirit of the fear of the Lord."

Of this consolation Protestantism deprives you, for it rejects the Sacrament of Confirmation, and, instead of it, tells you to renew your promise to live like a Christian, without giving you any new strength to do so, and even whilst denying that you can do so at all. The last part of this assertion I have proved above, and shall more fully prove in the sequel. Why, indeed, should man be strengthened by Divine grace, if, as genuine Protestantism teaches, he has no free-will and cannot merit before God? ? ? ?

III. THE HOLY EUCHARIST.

A true Christian loves his Redeemer. Like St. Augustine, he wishes to have lived in the time of Christ, to have been permitted to see Him, accompany Him, live near Him. Christ Himself said, "Blessed are your eyes, because they see, and your ears, because they hear." Who would not wish to have been one of His chosen disciples, or to have been allowed, like Mary, to live under the same roof with the incarnate Son of God for thirty years? Whoever loves Jesus as his Redeemer and his God, cannot help wishing that He were still on earth. Would I were with Him and He with me. Would I could fall at His sacred feet, like St. Mary Magdalene, and, when forgiven, speak with Him face to face, like a child with its father, like a friend with his friend, like one rescued from death with his deliverer, like a criminal to his judge, on whose sentence his liberty and life depend.

All this is realized in the Catholic Church. The Catholic doctrine is, that, under the sacramental veils, Jesus Himself is present, in the same flesh and blood, the same Divinity and Humanity, as when He lay a new-born infant in the manger, as when He rested on the lap of Mary, as when He labored with Joseph at Nazareth, as when He instructed the people, and entered Jerusalem in triumph: the same God-Man, who now sits in the highest heaven, at the right hand of God the Father, adored as the Lamb of God by all the angels and saints. Wherever there is a tabernacle in a Catholic church, in which a consecrated Host is kept, there Jesus is personally present. This is an ineffable consolation for a heart that loves Jesus, and longs to be with Him: the real presence of Jesus Christ makes a heaven of every Catholic church on the whole earth.

When the Jews wept for grief at the sight of the second Temple, the prophet Aggeus consoled them by the promise, that the presence of the Redeemer would render the glory of the second Temple greater than that of the first. Yet the presence of Jesus in the second Temple was to be but momentary. His permanent presence communicates an immeasurably higher degree of majesty and holiness to our churches, and, indeed, renders our poorest log chapels as venerable as the dome erected by the genius of Michael Angelo. Whether the Catholic kneels on a tesselated floor, or on the bare ground, he finds a never-failing source of consolation in communing with Jesus in the Blessed Sacrament.

In the old Temple, there was nothing holier than the Ark of the Covenant; still, the high priest alone was allowed to enter the Holy of Holies, and that only once a year. In Catholic churches, our Redeemer Himself dwells personally; we are all allowed and invited to come near Him, every day and every hour, and to converse with Him face to face.

The cloud which came down into the first Temple at its dedication, filled Solomon and all the people with the most consoling feelings of confidence, awe, and adoration: the Catholic, kneeling with a lively faith* and a loving spirit before the sacred species that conceal his Saviour, is filled with far more consoling sentiments of adoration, filial fear, and confidence, towards Him who thus deigns to dwell with men forever.

Jesus in the Blessed Sacrament was prefigured by the cloud which stood between the camp of Israel and the camp of the Egyptians, illumining the night for the Israelites, and serving as their guide to the land of promise. Moses might well say to the people, "Neither is there any nation so great, that hath gods so nigh them, as our God is present to all our petitions." The Israelites had but the figure; we enjoy the reality; we enjoy the literal accomplishment of the promise of our Lord, "Behold I am with you all days, even unto the consummation of the world."

Of this heavenly consolation Protestantism has utterly deprived you. Protestantism maintains that Jesus is no longer on earth. Open all your meeting-houses and churches, and show us where He is. He is not there: He has gone from amongst you never to return, for you acknowledge no priesthood, and have no one amongst you vested with the power of Consecration. You may build churches broader than St. Peter's, towers higher than the towers of Fribourg, Strasburg, and Vienna: they will be, after all, but empty houses, idle shows of grandeur, desolate, cheerless, chilling piles of stone, for He, on whom the beauty, the life, the inspiration of a Christian church depend, Jesus our Saviour does not dwell in your churches. It is infinitely more pleasant to worship kneeling on the bare floor, where our Lord is present, than to be seated in velvet-cushioned pews in your most sumptuous church edifices.

But, besides the Real Presence, the doctrine of Transubstantiation brings along with it other ineffable consolations. Jesus, under the species of bread and wine, is also the Sacrifice of the New Law, and the food of our souls.

A Christian, who truly loves his Saviour, would esteem it an unspeakable favor to have been permitted to stand near the Cross on Calvary, with Mary the Mother of God and with St. John; or to embrace the Cross, like Mary Magdalene, and weep for his sins whilst Christ was dying to redeem sinners. The Sacrifice of the Cross is to the Gospel what the sun is to the world; it is the source and the centre of our Religion. To that Sacrifice all generations of old looked forward for their deliverance. In that Sacrifice the Christian Church had her origin; from it, under the symbol of water and blood, gushed forth all the graces of Christianity; in it our faith, our hope, the life of our souls take their birth and have their sustenance.

Is there a Christian traveler, no matter how weak his faith, who, on visiting Jerusalem and the church of the holy Sepulchre, and standing on the ground where the Cross once stood, has not felt his love for Jesus quickened and his sorrows lightened? There are not a few among you, who have traveled to Jerusalem, and can bear witness that such were their impressions: indeed several among you have published their testimony of it to the world Never yet, said an American traveler some time ago, had I bent my knee in prayer; never yet had a tear of devotion moistened my eye: but when I came to the hallowed ground where my Saviour once hung bleeding on the Cross, I was forced to bend the knee; I sank down upon the floor, and wept.

Catholics need not travel so far to experience far more consoling emotions. Wherever there is an altar on which the Sacrifice of the Mass is offered, there is Calvary, there is the Cross, there is the Sacrifice of Calvary. Whoever understands the Catholic doctrine will easily conceive that a fervent Catholic must find in the Mass an unfailing source of the sweetest consolation.

The Catholic doctrine is, that the Mass is the same Sacrifice as the Sacrifice of Calvary; not that Christ dies again, but that He continues to offer forever, in an unbloody manner, the same Sacrifice of the Cross, which was the completion of all sacrifices. It is the fulfilment of the prophecy of Malachias: "From the rising of the sun even to the going down thereof, my name is great among the Gentiles, and in every place there is sacrifice, and there is offered to my name a clean oblation."*

* Malach., i. 10, 11.

The glorious worship of the blessed, the burning love of adoring seraphs, the adoration, praise, thanksgiving, love of all the hosts of heaven, since the dawn of their creation and throughout eternity, are as nothing to this Sacrifice of infinite value, to the adoration, thanksgiving, atonement, praise, intercession, love, which the incarnate Son of God Himself offers to His heavenly Father on our altars. With this worship, the only worship fully worthy of God, our own adoration is united, and made acceptable to God through Christ.

Thus the poorest Catholic Church on earth is like another heavenly Jerusalem, where the Lamb appears slain, as He appeared to St. John; the faithful on earth join their voices in the new canticle of heaven: "Worthy is the Lamb that was slain to receive power, and divinity, and wisdom, and strength, and honor, and glory, and benediction. Because Thou wast slain, and hast redeemed us to God, in Thy blood, out of every tribe, and tongue, and people, and nation."*

This Sacrifice throws over our service a light, a life, a majesty, a solemnity such as no other Religion can lay claim to. This is often felt and acknowledged even by Protestants,

* Apoc., v. 12, 9.

especially by such as are acquainted with the meaning of our impressive ceremonies, and understand how each rite refers to the great Victim on the altar.

This great Sacrifice of adoration, atonement, thanksgiving, and prayer, Christ offers for the salvation of all men, and of each one in particular, as truly as if each one was alone in the world. As often as he assists at Mass, a fervent Catholic draws new graces from the wounds of his Saviour sacrificed for him in his presence; a most consoling accomplishment of the prophecy: "You shall draw waters with joy out of the Saviour's fountains."*

Protestantism deprives you of this consolation. It denies the perpetuity of the Sacrifice of Christ, overthrows the altar, strips worship of its majesty, and despoils public service of the infinite merit which ours possesses in the Divine Sacrifice. Instead of altars, it gives you a bare pulpit; mere preaching and singing, instead of the great Sacrifice; the ministry of men alone, instead of the Real Presence of Christ. No wonder that your churches are not thronged like ours, nor visited for devotional purposes out of stated days and hours; or that they are even sometimes closed during a great

* Isa., xii. 3.

part of summer. Beyond the recognition that public worship is due to God, there is nothing in your religious meetings, which you may not have as well in your own houses, or even better. You assemble to hear a sermon; but you might read a sermon at home, and perhaps a better and a more edifying one, than the rant, or political discourses, containing not an allusion to religion, to which you are sometimes forced to listen, and which only disgust you or provoke you to anger. You pray and sing in common; but at home you might, perhaps, pray with less distraction, or with your families sing the praises of God with more devotion. Your churches lack what no devotion can supply, that which constitutes a church and distinguishes it from an ordinary building, the altar and the Divine Sacrifice.

In intimate connection with the Real Presence, we have our numerous religious Festivals; another great source of consolation to the Catholic. A Christian would wish to have been present at the great events wrought for his salvation. In the Catholic Church, his desire is fulfilled, as far as possible. The Catholic Church celebrates those glorious events, as if they were passing before our eyes, as you may see by reading the Catholic prayers, especially those in the Mass, appropriated to each

Festival. In this the Catholic Church conforms to the spirit of God, with whom there is neither yesterday, nor to-morrow, but an everlasting present.

With us the ecclesiastical year is like the tree of Paradise, laden with the richest fruits in all seasons, and always renewing the vigor of our faith, the freshness of our spiritual life.

Of all our beautiful festivals, you have hardly retained anything beyond a trace of their former existence among your Catholic ancestors. You celebrate Christmas, and perhaps Easter also, in your houses and at your tables more than in your churches. Such celebrations are not peculiarly Christian; in this country even Jews sometimes have a Christmas tree for their children. Your religious celebrations are cold indeed, when compared with the holy joy with which the Catholic Church celebrates the Festivals and seasons of Advent, Christmas, Easter, Pentecost, Corpus Christi All-Saints, All-Souls, and the days dedicated to our Lord or His blessed Mother. Most of these holy-days and seasons are common week-days among you. Whilst Catholics commemorate the mercies of God, and the mysteries of our Divine Lord's life, you are often laboring hard to amass what you cannot retain and reject consolations which would bear you fruit for eternity.

I now come to the greatest of all the consolations imparted by Christ through the Sacrament of the Holy Eucharist. A heart that loves Christ ardently, longs to be intimately united with Him, or even, like St. Paul, " desires to be dissolved and to be with Christ." It is true, the intimate union here referred to by St. Paul belongs only to heaven; but still, there is a union with Christ, possible on earth, more intimate than the human mind could have conceived, had it not been revealed.

It is the doctrine of the Catholic Church, that in Holy Communion Jesus enters our interior, really and substantially, body and soul, as God and Man, so that each one of us may say with the Apostle, "I live, now not I, but Christ liveth in me," not only by faith, but by the real presence of Christ within us. I need not stop to point out the numberless sweet consolations contained in this doctrine.

The Church teaches, that by Communion Jesus is united with us in so intimate a manner that human language is not adequate fully to express it. The holy Fathers often compare this union to the union of light with air or of heat with wax. They remark that Communion places in us the germ of immortality, and that the oftener and the more worthily we receive the Body and Blood of Christ, the greater will be our glory in heaven. Whoever receives Christ worthily, may say with the Spouse in the Canticles, "My beloved is mine, and I am his."

This consolation Protestantism denies you. It has, at best, left you but a shadow of Communion. The following are a few of its doctrines on this subject. Communion only signifies the Body of Christ; we only receive Christ by faith; the Body of Christ is really present, but only at the moment of Communion. This last opinion Protestants cannot consistently hold, for, admitting no Priesthood, they cannot claim any ministers having the power to change bread and wine into the Body and Blood of Christ. Whenever you partake of what is called among you the Lord's Supper, you receive bread and wine, nothing more. No wonder your Communion gives you no consolation, and that few among you care to receive it. Nothing is gained by receiving it, nothing lost by abstaining from it. What you should lament as one of your greatest misfortunes, is the loss you have incurred by your separation from the Catholic Church, the loss of the Real Presence and of the true Catholic Communion, the supreme good of man on earth. Protestantism has robbed you of it, and left you, in this respect, no better off than infidels or Jews. "We have an altar, whereof they have no power to eat who serve the tabernacle."*

IV. PENANCE.

Man is conscious of his frailty. Loaded with guilt, stung with remorse, in dread of the judgments of God, a Christian who has fallen into mortal sin after his baptism, would surely be glad that Christ had instituted a secure means of obtaining pardon. A friend seeks relief by revealing his secret sorrows to his friend; the sick disclose their secret disorders to physicians; men apologize for their offences to each other; criminals sometimes, goaded on by remorse, give themselves up to public justice, or after being condemned, seek to unburden their conscience by a public confession. The advantages of a confession of faults to a friend who can advise and instruct us, were noticed even by Seneca and other pagan philosophers: so deeply is the principle of Confession seated in our nature. Nothing, indeed, can be imagined more in harmony with our

* Heb., xiii. 10.

frail nature, or more desirable, especially for a Christian, than Confession under proper safeguards. I have offended God. Would there were on earth some representative of Christ, to whom I might with safety confess my sins, and receive a sure pledge of Divine pardon ; a man whom I could trust as a friend, a guide, a father, the physician of my soul; whose counsels might aid me to persevere in virtue, and who would never, under any circumstances reveal any of my failings.

The wish is fulfilled in the Catholic Church. Like the rainbow after the Deluge, the Sacrament of Penance is a sign and a pledge of reconciliation between God and repentant sinners.

By the Sacrament of Penance, sins are truly forgiven : the condition of pardon is Confession, accompanied by a sincere contrition and a firm resolution of amendment. The Confessor is the representative of Christ, the friend, guide, father, and physician of our souls. Such is the doctrine of the Catholic Church, founded on the explicit words of Christ : " Receive ye the Holy Ghost. Whose sins you shall forgive, they are forgiven them, and whose sins you shall retain, they are retained."*

* John, xx. 22, 23.

Words cannot be more decisive. "If there is any thing Divine in the Catholic Church," says Leibnitz, though himself a Protestant, "it is Confession, or the Sacrament of Penance."

Catholics are certain that the sins which they confess will never be revealed. The lips of the Priest are sealed, and the seal cannot be broken. Under no circumstances can a Priest disclose what he has heard in Confession. After Confession, he cannot even speak with the penitent of the sins he has confessed, without the penitent's express permission. You know how completely the secret of Confession is kept: you have had public proofs of it in your courts of law.

A Protestant traveler in Italy had always believed that Priests do not keep the secret of Confession. While at Rome, he determined to obtain a positive proof of his opinion. Having managed to get a certificate of ordination, which had belonged to a Priest, he put on the ecclesiastical dress, went to a church, and asked for a Confessor. He accused himself of saying Mass without being ordained, and declared that he would continue to do so, as it was the means by which he made his living. The Priest, of course, refused him absolution. The Protestant then following him to the sacristy, asked leave to say Mass, which the Priest, after having examined his papers, gave him without hesitation. The Priest with his own hand prepared the chalice and the vestments. For a moment, the Protestant looked on in silent astonishment, and then exclaimed, " Now I see undeniably that Priests do keep the secret of Confession. I want to be a Catholic." He was received into the Church, and soon experienced the consolation of having made a real Confession.

Protestantism deprives you of this consolation, for it rejects Confession, and holds that it is enough to confess to God. But where is it written that this is sufficient? Why has Christ said, " Whose sins you shall forgive, they are forgiven; and whose sins you shall retain, they are retained?" " Were these words of Christ spoken to no purpose," asks St. Augustine, " and are the keys which Christ has given to the Church, without power, that you should say, I confess only to God?" Would it not have been unworthy of Christ to have made use of the solemn ceremony of breathing upon His Apostles, and to have given them the Holy Ghost, with power to forgive or to retain sins, if, after all, He meant to give no such power? Would it not have been equally unworthy of the Divine Intelligence to have given them a discretionary power to remit or to retain sins, and not to have obliged Christians to a full confession of their sins, which is the only means to determine whether the sins are to be forgiven or to be retained? Then the words of Christ, would only have amounted to this: Receive ye the Holy Ghost to no purpose; receive ye the power to forgive or to retain sins, to no purpose, for no one, after all, need apply to you to be forgiven: it is enough for men to confess to God. Who would think of attributing such a grant to our Lord? And how could Confession have the advantages to which I have referred above, if we do not open our conscience fully to the Confessor, as to a physician, guide, friend, and father?

Let me relate an incident which happened some years ago in Paris. A Protestant lady, married to a Catholic Count, always noticed in him a peace of mind and heart to which she was a total stranger. On asking him the cause of it one day, she received for answer, "I am a Catholic, and Catholics can open their hearts to the Priest, the Representative of Christ. Confession is the cause of my peace." Not long after, one evening, when her mind was more disturbed than ever, the Countess sent for a Priest, and expressed a desire of making her confession to him. Finding that she was a Protestant, the Priest told her he could not comply with her request, because, as a Protestant, she was incapable of receiving absolution. She became a Catholic, and found in Confession that peace of conscience which she had been unable to account for in her husband.

I have been a Priest and Missionary for many years, and have heard several hundred thousand Confessions. Nowhere have I witnessed such signs of consolation as in the confessional. Often at the moment of absolution, the delight of being again reconciled to God, so overpowers the penitents, that, amidst sobs and tears, their hearts seem ready to break with excess of joy. I grieve to think that mere prejudice prevents you from enjoying a similar consolation.

A man once came to me in a rage, and asked whether it was true that I had induced his daughter to make a general Confession. I replied, "My dear sir, Priests do not answer such questions. But I should think that you must have ten times more need of making a good general Confession." This answer made him still more furious. "Calm yourself sir," I continued. "Do you know what a

OF PROTESTANTISM. 55

general Confession is? Have you ever made one?" "No, sir." "Then I will tell you. A general Confession is the confession of all the sins of your whole life from your childhood up to this hour. I do not know you, but I cannot help thinking that many things must be heavy on your heart. How old are you?" "Forty-eight." "Well, sir, how easy it would be for you to cast off the burden of forty-eight years, and have it buried in the abyss of God's infinite mercy by a sincere Confession." For a few moments he was silent and thoughtful, and then said, "You are right. When can I make my Confession?" I took him immediately to the church. He went home another man, grateful, and with joy depicted on his countenance.

If Methodists sometimes pretend to a similar sentiment of forgiveness, it is only a temporary delusion. The sentiment is merely personal, not warranted by any Sacrament or sign instituted by Christ. If they spoke sincerely, they would confess, that they themselves cannot rely on the feeling, as remorse invariably returns soon with as much keenness as ever. Even, if they could believe themselves forgiven, they could not, on Protestant principles, believe in any thing more than a mere covering of guilt and freedom from punishment, not a real cleansing of the soul. There is no consolation in reconciliation without true forgiveness, and guilt that remains on the soul must continue to burden and torment it.

Indulgences.—It is a Catholic doctrine, that, though truly absolved from sin and eternal pains, we often remain subject to temporal punishments for our sins: this is a check on relapse, worthy of the Divine Wisdom, and tempers Mercy with Justice. Nathan, after saying to David, "The Lord hath taken away thy sin, thou shalt not die," added, "Nevertheless, because thou hast given occasion to the enemies of the Lord to blaspheme for this thing, the child that is born to thee shall surely die."* Like David, we should wish to be freed, if possible, even from the temporal punishment, or to make up for it by meritorious works.

The Catholic Church teaches, that the temporal punishment can be made up for by meritorious works, or remitted by Indulgences. To gain a plenary Indulgence, it is an indispensable condition, as every Catholic knows, to be truly contrite and fully resolved to amend one's life, so as not to harbor any wilful attachment to a

* 2 Kings, xii. 13, 14.

single sin. Hence Indulgences are, also, a powerful means of Christian perfection.

Protestantism deprives you of this consolation, and this powerful means of virtue. It rejects Indulgences, and denies that the Catholic Church can grant them; as if Christ had not said, "Whatsover you shall loose upon earth, shall be loosed also in heaven;" and as if the power of forgiving sins,—" Whose sins you shall forgive, they are forgiven them,"— did not include the inferior power of remitting the temporal punishment due to sin.

It is to be deeply regretted, that many Protestant ministers are, especially on this subject, constantly doing all they can to distort the Catholic doctrine, and render it odious. They never cease repeating, that to grant Indulgences is to grant an unbounded license to sin, though every Catholic child could inform them, that to gain an Indulgence and to sin, are as incompatible as truth and falsehood, as heaven and hell. The Catholic doctrine is, that out of the state of grace, there is no Indulgence whatever, and that a perfectly pure heart, is necessary for gaining a plenary Indulgence. That a Protestant should reject Indulgences we can easily conceive: to be consistent with himself he must do so. Not believing a real conversion possible, he does not believe in Purgatory; he fears Hell alone.

V. EXTREME UNCTION.

A Christian, if true to his vocation, lives, not for fleeting time, but for eternity, which is rapidly drawing nigh. His chief care is to die well, to end his life in the friendship of God. He remembers his last end, and the warning of the Holy Ghost, "If the tree fall to the south or to the north, in what place soever it shall fall, there shall it be."* He remembers that " all is well, that ends well," that eternity depends on his last struggle, heaven or hell on his death. Not one of us fully knows what it is to die, but we all feel a natural repugnance to death; while the Christian is assured that, in our last moments, Satan does his worst to overpower us, and draw us with him into eternal ruin.

In that last and awful struggle, the soul needs extraordinary assistance. Has Christ given to His Church any such extraordinary assistance?

The Catholic Church teaches that He has done so in the Sacrament of Extreme Unction

* Eccle., xi. 3.

That Sacrament has a twofold effect, one on the body, and another on the soul.

In regard to the body, it confers relief, or perfect recovery. Facts are constantly occurring which bear witness to this efficacy, as promised by St. James: "Is any man sick among you, let him bring in the priests of the church, and let them pray over him anointing him with oil, in the name of the Lord: and the prayer of faith shall save the sick man, and the Lord shall raise him up, and if he be in sins, they shall be forgiven him."* Even Protestant and Infidel physicians have often acknowledged the efficacy of Extreme Unction in this respect. In Catholic countries they are anxious that the sick should receive the last Sacraments in due time, because they find that the repose which results from the reception of Extreme Unction, serves to give efficacy to the medicine which the sick person receives.

The spiritual effects of this Sacrament are still more certain and immediate. According to the Catholic doctrine, it removes the remaining effects of sin, and fortifies the soul in its last struggle.

Protestants, on visiting their sick Catholic friends, are frequently convinced by their own

---

* James, v. 14, 15.

observations, of the wonderful calm and fortitude imparted by Extreme Unction to the dying. Catholic Priests frequently meet with Protestants in hospitals, who are converted to Catholicity, by the evident efficacy of Extreme Unction. It has often happened, in the course of my ministry, especially while I attended the Commercial Hospital in Cincinnati, that Protestant patients called and entreated me to give them Extreme Unction. They had witnessed the extraordinary peace and strength of mind which descended from Heaven on their Catholic fellow-sufferers, at the moment they received that Sacrament; and many Protestants, from their desire of receiving the last consolations of the Catholic Church, became Catholics on their death-beds.

This reminds me of another fact still more remarkable, and, by itself alone, going far to prove that the Catholic Church is the true Church, and that earnest and sincere inquirers, acknowledge it as such, as soon as they overcome, with the Divine assistance, the prejudices of education, habit, and public opinion. Hundreds, I might say thousands, of Protestants become Catholics in the last awful nour, when illusions vanish and things appear as they are. There are few Priests engaged in the ministry, who cannot testify to this from their own experience. Now, Americans, I would ask you, and I would ask all the Protestants in the world, whether they have ever heard or known of a Catholic becoming a Protestant on his death-bed? I never have; and neither you nor your descendants to the end of time shall ever know or hear of a *single one*.

The Catholic Church enjoins it on her ministers, as a strict duty, to assist the dying with the most loving care, the most watchful solicitude, the tenderest zeal of which they are capable. You know the heroic zeal of our Priests; the whole country has witnessed it in times of cholera and yellow fever. No sooner does a Catholic fall dangerously ill, no matter how contagious his disease, than the Priest hastens to his bedside, and, if possible, remains with him to the last moment. He stands by his side, like a consoling angel at the threshold of eternity, whispering confidence in God's mercy, until the soul takes its flight, and then, following it with the prayers and blessings of the Church, in her name he invites the angels and the saints to descend and accompany the departed soul to heaven.

Protestantism deprives you of this consolation. It rejects Extreme Unction and all our last consoling ministrations. Just at the moment when the aid of the Church is most needed, you are forsaken : your ministers can give you no comfort but that of exhorting you —to help yourselves. Many of you have experienced it, all have witnessed it, and none of you expect any thing better. I ask you, Americans, when an epidemic breaks out among you, who are amongst the first to secure their safety by flight? Is it not very frequently your ministers? And who are the first to hasten, even from a distance, to places infected by the contagion? Is it not Catholic Priests, and Catholic Sisters of Charity? Ask Norfolk, New Orleans, and other cities ; every man in them will tell you.

VI. HOLY ORDERS.

A Christian who has a lively faith in the Church and in the dignity of her sanctuaries, in the Divinity of her Sacrifice and the holiness of her Sacraments, feels the propriety and necessity of intrusting sacred things to sacred hands. The ancient Pagans, obeying the instinct of our common nature, had a Priesthood set aside for their temples. Under the Old Law, though the Mosaic rites and sacrifices were only figures of things to come, yet God had set apart one of the twelve tribes for the service of the Temple, and had chosen, out of this tribe, one family, which was empowered to offer up sacrifice. In the Catholic Church, the holiness of the sanctuary demands far more imperatively, that an order of men should be consecrated to serve at the altar and administer the Sacraments. The highly responsible offices of the Priest, require likewise that he should receive special graces for the faithful discharge of his duties.

Has Christ provided for this? The Catholic Church answers that He has done so in the Sacrament of Holy Orders.

The solemn and sublime ceremonies of a Catholic Ordination are in complete harmony with the solemn duties and sublime ministry of the Priest. I wish all of you could witness a Catholic Ordination. It would leave on your minds an impression of sanctity, which years could not efface. Every prayer, every rite in a Catholic Ordination has a deep significance, and, indeed, breathes a superhuman majesty and a heavenly spirit: the unction of the Holy Spirit is diffused throughout the whole. The newly ordained Priest, often perceptibly, eels the affluence of Divine grace pervade his whole being, making his Ordination felt, and rendering him vividly conscious of the new power with which he is invested. He has always the assurance of actual graces that will enable him to be true to his vocation, and becomes conscious, in a manner which he could not have anticipated, that he was chosen from amongst his people, like Aaron, and has become a representative of Christ on earth, a mediator between Him and men, a priest, teacher, shepherd, friend, and father of His people.

In accordance with his high dignity, is the life of continence, which the Church imposes upon the Priest. That life perfects in him the image of Christ, who, as St. Paul says in his Epistle to the Hebrews,* is a High Priest according to the order of Melchisedech, without father, mother, or genealogy. By his life of continence, and by it only, the Priest is able, without any domestic care to impede his action, to make himself all things to all men, to become the spiritual father in Christ of all his congregation, and to command in an unexceptionable manner their full confidence.

Protestantism refuses you the consolation of

* Heb., v. 10; vii. 3.

having ministers thus sanctified and absolutely set apart for the Divine ministry, for Protestantism rejects Holy Orders. Its ministers are without any higher than a mere human ordination and a mere human authority. Their mission, like that of civil officers, emanates from men, not from God. A Protestant minister is the minister or agent of his congregation: they pay him for his services, and dismiss him when it suits them. If he gives up his profession, he becomes a mere layman. His station, compared with the exalted position of the Catholic Priest, looks worldly, common, and low indeed.

As Protestant ministers acquire no essentially new character in their ordination, so as to be forever distinct from laymen, every one may be admitted to the ministry. Very often, especially in this country, in the comparatively numerous sect of Methodists, we find merchants, farmers, carpenters, blacksmiths, artisans of every trade, assuming the office of preachers on Sunday, and returning to their usual avocations for the rest of the week; and that not only in country towns and districts, but in the largest cities of the Union.

No wonder Protestantism enjoins on its ministers no mode of life above that of laymen

But the consequence is, that, being burdened with wives and children, Protestant ministers become a burden to their congregations, and take more care of their household, as they are in duty bound to do, than of their flocks. I have read in a newspaper a complaint of an Episcopalian Bishop, that he either had to apply for a divorce, or give up the idea of making episcopal visitations, as his wife's jealousy would not allow him to absent himself from home.

VII. MATRIMONY.

As the Priest holds the position of spiritual father to the Christian people, and needs particular graces to fulfil the peculiar duties and meet the peculiar difficulties of his position; so parents require special graces in the duties and difficulties pertaining to their condition.

The Christian who is called to the state of Matrimony, feels the necessity, and desires the grace of this Sacrament, for on his conduct in Marriage depends his happiness or his misery in time and in eternity.

Has Christ provided any special grace for the state of Matrimony? The Catholic Church answers that He has done so by raising Matrimony to the dignity, and giving it the efficacy, of a Sacrament. This state which would seem altogether worldly, has been spiritualized and sanctified: indeed, Christ has so exalted it as to make it the symbol of his own union with the Church.

Thus the grace of the Redemption, as understood by the Catholic Church, reaches to every condition of life, and sanctifies and exalts them all.

Another point of Catholic doctrine, which goes further still to sanctify Marriage, and powerfully tends to make husband and wife regard each other with a holy awe, is the indissolubility of the bond of Matrimony: the married couple are united for life, as Christ is united with His Church for eternity. Thus the whole state of the Christian family is sanctified.

Protestantism deprives married persons and the family of this consolation, for it rejects Matrimony as a Sacrament. In the Protestant view, the matrimonial contract is only a civil act, and Matrimony nothing more than a union of man and wife in the natural order. Hence, Protestantism permits divorce and sanctions new alliances, thus paving the way to unrestrained licentiousness, by furnishing the vicious with an easy means of uniting with other parties, whenever passion prompts them to do so. Hence, stripped of all its Christian sanctity, Matrimony but too frequently becomes a source of scandal. Cases have been made public, in which women, after having had five or six husbands, in consequence of repeated divorces, at last returned to their first husband after a new divorce. Does not Marriage, in this way, come to have more the character of a brutal connection, than of a Christian alliance?

Indeed, Protestantism seems but too much inclined to sanction even polygamy, as was actually done by the Baptists in Luther's time, and by Luther himself, along with Melanchthon and Bucer, when these founders of Protestantism gave leave to the Landgrave Philip of Hesse to have two wives at the same time. Mormonism, too, is one of the *noble* plants grown in the hotbed of Protestantism.

GOOD WORKS.

By the grace of the Sacraments, and by the actual graces of the Holy Ghost, a Catholic feels himself strong enough to resist every temptation, able to overcome all obstacles to virtue, to become more virtuous every day more and more like to Christ by the daily practice of good works, to increase in merit before God, every hour and moment, and to gain an ever increasing crown of glory by his merits. This is truly a great consolation for a man who loves God, and is desirous of improving in virtue. "I can do all things in Him who strengtheneth me."* I can do all things, if I only have the *will* to follow Christ with the fervor of the Saints. If I only have the will, " my present tribulation, which is momentary and light, will work in me above measure an exceeding weight of glory."

Protestantism deprives you of this consoling and powerful motive for practicing virtue, by teaching you that you can do no good works at all, even with the aid of Divine grace, and that what appears right in your eyes is a sin before God.

Many among you, unacquainted with the original doctrines of Protestantism, and Protestants only in name, may be disposed to accuse me of calumny. To prove my assertion, I make some quotations from the works of the early Reformers. Luther says, "Every good work, though performed as well as possible, is still a venial sin."† " Yea, every action of the just man is damnable and a mortal sin."‡

---

* Philipp., iv. 4.
† Assert. Omn. Art. Opp. Tom. II., p. 325.
‡ Cp. Antilatom. (Confut. Luther. Rat. latom.) fol. 406, 407,

Melanchthon is just as explicit. He says, "All our actions and exertions are sins."* "Yea, even to eat, to drink, to work, to teach, all this is sin."† Calvin teaches the same doctrine: "Never yet has a pious person done a pious work, which was not damnable in the sight of God."‡

How, with such a prospect before them, can men have any zeal for Christian sanctity or genuine virtue? The certainty of offending God by our best works, must inevitably deaden and destroy, in the very root, every desire for virtue. The doctrine, if generally acted on, must sweep every vestige of virtue from the earth. In all cases, when adhered to in any degree, it is enough to sadden and deject, and degrade in his own estimation, every honest man, who believes in God and longs to be pleasing in His sight.

If you ask the Reformers, What hope can a man have of saving his soul, if he is not able to do any thing towards saving it? You promise him salvation, and command him to hope; but on what ground is his hope to rest?

---

* Melanchth. Loc. Theol., p. 108.
† Ibid, p. 92.
‡ Calvin. Instit. l. II. c. viii. § 59; l. III. c. iv. § 28, and c. xiv. § 11.

The early Reformers answer, and consistent Protestants at the present day agree with them, that man, as he is thoroughly wicked, can only be saved by faith. If he has the faith, sin cannot injure him, and he has no need of good works. Some of you may put this down as an unheard of calumny, and indignantly ask me when and where the Reformers ever uttered such abominable doctrines.

Open Luther's works, for instance his "*De Captivitate Babylonica,*" and you will find this doctrine taught and inculcated.* In a letter to Melanchthon, his friend and co-Reformer, he uses the following language: "Sin as much as you can, but believe still more firmly. We must sin as long as we live. It is enough to believe firmly in Christ, the Lamb of God, who taketh away the sins of the world. From Him sin will not separate us, were we to commit murder and adultery a thousand times a day.†

Some of Luther's followers went so far as to assert that good works are dangerous to salvation, on the false ground that they impair the saving confidence of faith. Nicholas Amsdorf,

---

* De Captiv. Babyl. l. II., p. 26.
† Epist. Dr. Mart. Luth. a Joan. Aurifabro collectæ tom. I. Jena, 1556.

an old friend of Luther's, maintained this, in the year 1559, as genuine Lutheran doctrine.* The doctrine is held by some Calvinist Protestants to this day. Some time ago, I met with one who defended it, a Swiss Calvinist preacher, with whom I happened to travel to St. Louis. As regards Americans, I hope there is not one among them who takes such abominable views of the Christian Religion. Yet it must always remain true that the Reformers inculcated them as the pure doctrine of Christ; and, with such leaders, Protestantism must, to say the least, look exceedingly suspicious.

THE STATE OF MAN AFTER DEATH.

PURGATORY.

Our life on earth will soon be past, and eternity will quickly begin for us. A Christian may not be conscious of any mortal sin unatoned for, yet he knows that the eye of God discovers imperfections even in His saints; he feels that he is not worthy of Christ, and has no resource except in God's infinite mercy, and

* Cfr. Calv. Instit. l. III. c. 12. 86. Item Luther. Do Cfr. Bab. l. ii., p. 284, and Edit. Lips. l. xiv., p. 128.

in the hope that, if he has not reached stainless perfection here, God will purify his soul in a future state.

The Catholic Church affirms that his hope is not a vain one. She teaches that there is a place of expiation, called Purgatory, where souls are perfectly cleansed from every stain of sin ; and further, that the souls in Purgatory remain united with the living in the bonds of a holy love, and that this union is a real and efficacious, not a fruitless, union ; that the suffering souls are relieved, and even released, in view of our intercessions and good works, and especially by the Sacrifice of the Mass. The Catholic Church teaches, besides, that those souls, grateful for our assistance, intercede for us in their turn, especially after their admittance into heaven.

It is a great consolation to be able to give such efficacious proofs of our love to our departed friends. It lessens our sorrow for their loss ; it strengthens Christian hope in us, and permits us to taste all its sweetness. It has, besides, the highly beneficial effect of frequently fixing our thoughts on our last end and an impending eternity. The Holy Ghost has said, " It is a holy and wholesome thought to pray for the dead that they may be loosed fron sin."* All experience shows that it is both holy and consoling.

 I question whether more consoling tears are ever shed, than those that flow in prayer over the graves of the departed. Ask a loving son, or daughter, when they rise from their knees at the graves of their parents; ask a widow or mother bending in tears over the tombstone of a husband or son, whether any thing on earth has power to console them, half as much as prayer for the departed. Indeed, merely to see others praying at the graves of their relatives and friends, is enough to make us share, by Christian sympathy, in the visible consolation that refreshes the mourners.

Protestantism takes away this consolation. It denies Purgatory, declares prayers for the dead useless, and stigmatizes them as superstitious. It leaves the full bitterness of death rankling in the hearts of the survivors. Besides, the Protestant doctrine contradicts all just notions of merit and punishment, and entangles you in a net of inconsistencies. For if there is no Purgatory, a man who dies without being in mortal sin, yet not without failings, cannot go to Heaven, nor yet can he be con

---

* 2 Mach., xii. 46.

demned to Hell, since nothing defiled can enter Heaven, and it would be injustice in God to condemn a man to Hell who is not guilty of any grievous transgressions. Whither then shall he be sent?

On this point, an infidel could convict Protestantism of error. If you admit Heaven and Hell, he might say, you are forced either to admit Purgatory, or to maintain that the slightest failing is a mortal sin deserving Hell. The Reformers, as we have seen, maintained the latter alternative. But I greatly doubt whether any of you are ready to go so far, and would say that every slight fault, such as a useless word, or a momentary irritation, is a grievous sin and deserves eternal punishment. Every intelligent man must come to the conclusion that there is a middle place. Infidels would sooner deny the existence of Hell than that of Purgatory. In fact, the Universalists do so, and many modern Protestants agree with them, for the Hell which they admit not being eternal, is nothing more than Purgatory. The denial of Purgatory is as inconsistent with reason as it is distressing. It is as repugnant to the mind as to the heart, to think that our departed friends, whom we cannot believe to have been without failings, are all lost, and beyond the reach of our prayers.

THE COMMUNION OF SAINTS.

As Christians we believe that all who are free from sin at the moment of death, enter Heaven. We should naturally wish to remain in communion with them, if possible; to make them acquainted with our wants and sorrows, and receive from them some efficacious assistance, just as we remain in communication with our friends in distant countries, and are united with them in feeling, affection, and mutual services.

The Catholic Church affirms that there exists a Communion between us and the blessed; that the Saints know our wants, sympathize in our joys and sorrows, and pray for us, because they love us. They have reached the haven, and now extend a helping hand to their brethren still on the stormy ocean. We might, of course, pray to God alone, but God, in his infinite wisdom and love, has united all his children, in time and in eternity, in the bonds of a mutual, intimate, active, efficacious love. This is the order of Divine Providence. As we pray for the souls in Purgatory, so the Saints in

Heaven intercede for us, and the prayers of all are efficacious. This beautiful Communion with the Saints carries along with it the recollection of their virtues, and warns us to secure a part in their glory for ourselves by imitating their example.

There is in this Communion of holy love a consolation which all must acknowledge. Wherever faith exists, consolation is sought in mutual prayer. We ask each other's prayers, and find a comfort in the thought that those who love us pray for us and with us. Virtuous parents and children are consoled by knowing that each fulfils his duty of holy love by praying for the other. The consolation of Catholics often exhibits itself visibly, when a Priest promises to remember them at the altar. The Apostle himself asked the prayers of the newly converted; and the early Christians were united in the joys of mutual prayer, as well as in mutual love. There is a mutual consolation even in death, when parents can close their eyes with the assurance that their children will pray for them, and when children hear from the dying lips of their parents the parting promise to remember them before God in heaven. There is a consolation for all the faithful in the thought, that in losing a brother or dear-loved friend on earth, they gain an affectionate intercessor in heaven.

To be united to the Saints in heaven, to be one heart and one soul with them, is a consolation great in proportion to the purity, and power, and glory of the Saints. The balmy breath of a pure life is wafted from the highest heaven into our inmost souls; glorious witnesses watch our struggles, powerful protectors cover us with their shields, victorious heroes spur us on to victory by their example.

Saints, in the strictest sense of the word, those whose heroic virtues God has attested by manifest miracles, are a source of consolation peculiar to the Catholic. Protestants are often forced to acknowledge and admire the greatness of their virtues. They all belong to us: Protestants claim none of their own. We possess, as I have remarked above, a countless host of Saints, virgins, confessors, priests, bishops, martyrs. To be of the same Church with these numberless heroes of the Cross, to be in intimate, active, efficacious Communion with them, this, assuredly, is an exceedingly great consolation.

Of all this consolation Protestantism has utterly despoiled you. It denies our Communion with the Saints, maintains that the

Saints neither know our wants nor hear our prayers, and even pretends that their prayers for us would be an injury to Christ. Protestantism has forgotten, or does not wish to remember, what faith so explicitly teaches, that all that the Saints are, and all they are able to do for us, they are, and are able to do, only in and through Christ. All the children of Christ, whether living or dead, whether on earth or in heaven, are united in Him, one in Him through love, and this intimate union with each other, is brought home to us in the Communion of Saints. Protestantism breaks up the consoling union of the children of God, removes the Saints from us to an unapproachable region, and leaves no trace of a living, active Communion between the Church on earth and the Church in heaven. Death, if we would believe Protestantism, ends all Communion between brethren. The dead are dead, is the climax of the icy, deathlike, and deadening doctrines of Protestant theology.

Here I close my comparison. Whoever has given the preceding pages an attentive perusal, will, I hope, acknowledge that I have fully made out the charge that Protestantism is a

Religion of Distress, that it has rejected the consoling doctrines of the Church, and substituted for them most distressing tenets. I am, therefore, justified in asking you with deep astonishment and unfeigned compassion, How could your ancestors reject the Catholic Church for such a Religion? How can their descendants have blindly clung to it for three centuries? You will agree, that, on the supposition of both the Catholic and Protestant doctrines being mere human inventions, there would be good reasons, founded on real wants, for becoming Catholics, but not a single valid reason for becoming Protestants.

A learned Protestant, Lessing, has said, "Considering the faith of a Catholic Priest, I can imagine no man happier than he must be." This is the truth. Happy, indeed, is he, and happy beyond the measure allotted to other men, who has been ordained to be the dispenser of the mysteries of grace under the New Law, and the representative of the mercies of Christ to men. I need only point to the privilege of offering up in real Sacrifice to God the Body and Blood of the Redeemer. If you conceive what a Catholic priest is, you must see that it is a surpassing consolation for a man purchased by the blood of Jesus, to be permitted to stand in so intimate a union with Him, and to offer such a Sacrifice for his own salvation and the salvation of the world. The Priest is placed on Calvary and near the Cross, in a manner given to none but him.

I shall say nothing of the consolations he derives from the administration of the other mysteries of grace, at whose source he stands. I will only remark, that Lessing might just as well have said, "Considering the faith of a *Catholic*, I cannot imagine a happier man than a practical Catholic." Lavater, another celebrated Protestant, said as much in his "Portable Library for Friends:" "I consider a practical Catholic as one of the most honorable and blessed of men." He is blessed indeed, for he enjoys in the certainty of his faith, in the infallibility of its promises, in the consolations it administers, that "peace of God, which surpasseth all understanding," which the world cannot give, and which Protestant sects desire, but seek in vain.

I here recall to mind a fact which happened at Milwaukie, during a renovation of the Mission. A physician, a man of education, followed me to my room after a sermon, and threw himself into an arm-chair in an evident state of despair. I asked him, "What do you want of me, sir." "Comfort, comfort," he answered, "I want consolation and peace, and cannot find it in my Religion." "What is your Religion?" "I am a Protestant." "Have you the courage to examine?" "Certainly." "Then you will soon be a Catholic, and find consolation." And so it proved.

Learned Protestants, such as Leibnitz, Claudius, Haman, Jacobi, Schiller, Goethe, Novalis, Wolfgang Menzel, seem to have anticipated the consolation which the Catholic religion would have given them. They longed for it, but had not the resolution to brave public opinion, and avail themselves of the consolations that would have secured their happiness here and hereafter.

It happened, while I lived at Vienna, that a celebrated Protestant minister mounted the pulpit on Good Friday, to preach a sermon on the Passion of our Lord. He said in a mournful tone of voice, "Ah, what a death, my brethren! I ought to comfort you, but alas! I myself have no consolation. Amen." Without adding another word, he left the pulpit. This theatrical display had but too much truth in it. The death of Christ has no power to comfort us, if we refuse to approach the streams of consolation that flow from it. That minister spoke as if standing in spirit on Calvary, and pronounced judgment against himself and against the whole system of Protestantism. Luther himself declared that " he had never derived any consolation from his new Religion, and that he could not draw any consolation from the death and resurrection of Christ, in consequence of his want of faith."*

Protestantism is, and must forever be, a Religion without consolation, a Religion of Distress. It appears such, especially, when its doctrines are compared with the doctrines of the Catholic Church.

The only consolation Protestantism as such has to offer, is a wicked one,—*Sin, but believe.* In thus stigmatizing Protestantism, and in all I have to add in conclusion of this portion of my subject, I do not mean to speak of Protestants in general, and least of all of modern Protestants, most of whom are Protestants only in name, and have never fully examined the genuine Protestant system as it came from the hands of the early Reformers. Whoever examines Protestantism in its origin, primitive direction, and logical developement, must come to the conclusion that it is only fit to console a

* Colloq. 1556, p. 104, and p. 135 Abendmahlslehre. Zweybruken, p. 404.

wicked heart: I believe, therefore I may sin as much as I please; sin can do me no harm, for with all the crimes in the world on my conscience, if I have faith, I am sure of heaven. This is the secret starting point of the Reformation, its real origin, and root; it gave birth to all the doctrines peculiar to Protestantism, and contains an obvious explanation of all it has rejected. The primitive Protestant principle once admitted, that a man may do all that he pleases, and still be saved, provided he believes, there is no longer any use for Confession, Indulgences, Extreme Unction, the Invocation of Saints, nor for any of the peculiar doctrines of the Catholic Church; the laws of God themselves are practically abolished.

The primitive Protestant principle, as it leads on the one hand to a wicked presumption of the mercy of God, and an unfounded hope of heaven, as its only consolation; so, on the other hand, it generates despair. Extremes meet. I have asserted, not only that Protestantism is a Religion of Distress, but that it is a Religion of Despair; this may be partly concluded from the preceding pages, and I now proceed to prove it more fully.

SECTION II.

CONSEQUENCES.

Protestantism leads to despair, because it denies free-will. This alone proves the assertion.

For a large number of Protestants, despair is the consequence likewise of the fundamental Protestant doctrine, that the Bible is the only Rule of Faith, and that every one must make out his own faith from the Bible, for no one can come to any certainty in regard to faith either by Private Interpretation or by Private Inspiration ; and for those who cannot read, or cannot succeed in imagining that they have any Private Inspiration, nothing evidently is possible but despair.

Luther himself confessed that he was tempted to despair. On one occasion, Dr. Jonas, in a conversation with him, quoted the text of St.

Paul, "For the rest, there is laid up for me a crown of justice," and exclaimed, "How beautifully the Apostle speaks!" "Yes," replied Luther, "but I do not think he believed as firmly as his words seem to indicate. People imagine that I believe as firmly, as I express myself strongly in my sermons; but that is not the case."* Indeed, Luther, not only confessed that he was tempted to despair, and that he was frequently so tempted, but he thought that St. Paul was tempted to despair as well as he, and in this sense he explained the words of the Apostle, "I die daily."

Protestantism has also advanced the doctrine of Predestination. Calvin taught explicitly that God, from all eternity, has predestined a portion of the human race to salvation, and the rest to eternal ruin. He says, "We call Pre-
"destination the eternal decree of God, by
"which He has ordained of His own free-will
"what He will do with every man, for all men
"are not created in the same manner, but
"some are appointed for eternal salvation,
"others for eternal damnation. Hence accord-
"ing as a man is created, we say that he is
"predestined either to eternal life, or to eternal
"damnation."† Calvin goes so far in this

* Luther. Colloq. p. 133.
† Calv. Institut. L III. c. 21. n. 9.

blasphemous doctrine, as to say, that "God "permits those who are predestined to eternal "damnation to do some good in this life, but "that He permits it only in order to make them "the more guilty and punish them the more 'severely in eternity."* Not only Calvinists, but all true Protestants, even such as do not hold Calvin's horrible axioms explicitly, are in consistency bound to admit the doctrine of absolute Predestination. This follows from the doctrine of Luther and his followers, admitted by all genuine Protestants, that the fall has completely ruined our nature, and, hence, destroyed our free-will. Salvation or damnation, therefore, cannot in any degree depend on free-will, for free-will does not exist; hence, it must depend absolutely on Divine Predestination, the more so, as, according to genuine Protestant doctrine, there is no such thing as co-operation with grace or with justification. The same consequence follows from the Protestant doctrine of saving faith, for, as taught by Protestantism, this saving faith no one can give to himself, or co-operate in obtaining.

Melanchthon agrees with Calvin, and says without hesitation, "Every thing that happens,

* Instit. l. III. c. 2. n. 11.

happens necessarily by Divine Predestination, therefore our will has no freedom."*

In opposition to this general Protestant doctrine, the Council of Trent has framed the following canon : " If any one shall say, that the grace of justification is given to those only who are predestined to life eternal ; but that all the others who are called, are called indeed, but receive no grace, because by Divine power predestined to evil ; let him be anathema."†

After this, my candid American friends, judge whether I have exaggerated my charges against Protestantism, considered, chiefly, in its origin and primitive direction. I hope I have torn away from the face of Protestantism the mask of a Divine Religion. It is not my fault if Protestantism now appears to you like a spectre, risen from its grave of three centuries of corruption, staring you in the face with the empty look of desolation, and welcoming you with the ghastly smile of despair.

ULTERIOR CONSEQUENCES.

But there is worse than despair in its unearthly aspect. Taking Protestantism in its

* Melanchth. Loc. Theol. edit. Augsb. 1821.
† Conc. Trid. Sess. vi. can. xvii.

origin and primitive direction, I have to brand it with a still darker stigma. On a more thorough investigation, you will discover in it abominations such as were shown to Ezechiel in the vision of the wall of Jerusalem. As with the prophet, who at first did not see any thing offensive, but, after digging into the wall, beheld the abominations of the city ; so it is with many Protestants, particularly with such as believe in Christ as the Redeemer of the world, and the Founder of a Divine Church. They only see in Protestantism a peculiar developement of Christianity, with nothing that strikes them as offensive. To hold that every man must make out his religion from his own Bible, does not seem to them to have in it any thing very alarming. But this is not the whole of Protestantism, nor Protestantism as such, that is, Protestantism considered in its origin, tendencies, and logical developements. It is only upon a closer examination than ordinary, that Protestants come to discover its real nature and entire meaning, and are forced to admit that it is odious in itself and abominable in its consequences. I will show you that Protestantism in its origin and logical tendencies, is a Religion of immorality, of insubordination and despotism, of irreligion and blasphemy.

You may feel indignant at these charges, and they must appear to you to be most atrocious calumnies; but before throwing away the book, glance at my proofs, and refute them if you can: this much I have a right to expec from your candor and independence of character.

I call Protestantism, in its origin and logical tendencies, a Religion of immorality. Here is my proof. Luther and his associates taught that Christ had abrogated the whole moral law; that the moral law was only to be regarded as a rule of policy for holding society together, but that, as a matter of conscience, the true believer need not trouble himself about it. Read Luther's "Commentaries on the Epistle to the Galatians," and you will find this very doctrine word for word. Among other things he has the following: "Therefore we say that the Ten Commandments have no right to accuse or frighten a conscience in which Christ reigns by His grace, as Jesus has annulled such a right in the Law." And again, "In general, Christ did not come to instruct mankind as a Teacher. This He has only done by chance. His office was only that of covering the sins of men."

This is what Luther and the other Reformers

understood, or pretended to understand, by the freedom of the Gospel. They all taught that the moral law can give no uneasiness to the conscience of the believer, because he has faith in Jesus, who by His merits has covered every transgression of the Law. Hence they say, " The Holy Ghost is principally called the Paraclete or Comforter, because He comforts the disquieted consciences of believers, by enlivening their faith, which renders every wound of conscience harmless."*

Luther calls Catholic Theologians fools, who do not know what they say, when they maintain that Christ has abrogated the ceremonies only of the Old Law, *not the Commandments.* In his " Commentary on the Epistle to the Galatians," he compares the sensual man to Abraham's mule left behind in the valley, while Abraham ascended Mount Moria with Isaac. He says, " The mule at the foot of the mountain could do what it pleased. So the minds of believers may without uneasiness sun themselves on the mountain, without troubling themselves with what the mule of the flesh may do."

The Ten Commandments are only an ex-

* Solid. Declar. V. De Lege et Evang.

planation of the natural law: abrogate them, and there is an end of all morality, and we need no longer talk of virtue. As is amply proved by the complaints of the early Reformers, the new gospel morality soon bore its fruit in the frightful licentiousness that spread far and wide even in their own lifetime.

Protestantism, in its origin, was so deeply infected with this kind of gospel freedom, that the contagion crossed the ocean and covered all England. The Methodist Conference, under Wesley, in 1770, declared publicly, that the reason of the fearful, universal immorality then prevailing, was the wide-spread opinion that " Christ had annulled the Moral Law, and that evangelical freedom dispensed with the Ten Commandments."

Many of the adherents of the Reformers, no doubt, spurned this wicked doctrine; and there is not, perhaps, a man among you who does not repudiate it with scorn and disgust. Still, as Protestants, you are the followers of the first Reformers, and honor them as your leaders The birth-place of those men, who receive so much of your praises, is still infected with the breath of their noisome teachings. How long will you endure a Religion of whose fundamental doctrines such teachings are the legitimate deductions? I say legitimate, for if man has no free-will, as Protestantism has maintained, he cannot be bound by any law, any more than the brute. Were you to discover that a single accredited Catholic theologian has ever taught that the Ten Commandments are not binding on the consciences of Catholics, I verily believe you would instantly drive us all out of the country. Why do you not turn against Protestantism, the same indignation that would be raised against us? Can that be right in the case of Protestants, which in the case of Catholics would be an atrocious crime?

I have called Protestantism, in its origin and logical tendency, a Religion of disorder and despotism. If the Divine law has no binding force, it is evident that human laws can have none. Whoever has a right to say, I am my own authority in faith, my own judge in Religion, my own master in Divine things, must be allowed to say, and have the courage to proclaim with no less boldness, I am my own Sovereign and my own law-giver, and will not be bound by the laws of the State. There is no need of being a Louis XIV.; it is enough to be a consistent reasoner, after you have once said, *I am the Church*, to take the next step and say, "*L' état c'est moi—I am the State.*" When once this step is taken, confusion, tumult violence, bloodshed, anarchy, must ensue ; or if they do not, it is because men are inconsistent, and afraid to carry out their opinions, to their full length, in practice. Indeed, you are, in general, much better men, than logicians. When Germany was deluged with blood by the rising of the peasants, Erasmus was right in writing to Luther, " We now reap the fruits of your spirit. You do not acknowledge the leaders, *but they acknowledge you.* You have, it is true, disowned their proceedings in your frantic little book, but you do not prove that you have given no occasion to the calamity by the books which you have written against monks and bishops, and concerning evangelical freedom."

Protestantism, in its origin, likewise established the principle, and furnished the justification of despotism. Luther says in his " Commentary on the Epistle to the Galatians," " Human laws have nothing to do with conscience." And writing about the Rebellion of the Peasants, he says, " Let cannons roar around the heads of the peasants ; these are the only reasons to be given to those fellows. It matters not if some innocent man perish in the conflict." This is a pretty despotic counsel

All know how faithfully it was followed by Henry VIII. and Elizabeth. "My Lords, either your consent, or your heads," said Henry VIII., to his stubborn Parliament, and then rubbed his hands together with quiet self-complacency. The original Protestant principles make the Sovereign a despot over the Church as well as in the State. You are acquainted, I hope, with the famous old Protestant axiom, "*Cujus est regio, illius est religio*—*He that rules the country is master of its religion.*" Even in our own days, a woman rules the Church of England as its supreme head. Some of your prejudiced historical writers continue to repeat the exploded fable of a *Johanna Papissa*—Pope Joan: in England, we have a real female pope in the person of Queen Victoria.

Lastly, I have called Protestantism, in its origin and logical tendency, a Religion of irreligion and blasphemy. I prove it. Where no free-will exists, there can exist no religious duties, and a Religion without religious duties is no Religion at all. A Religion that denies free-will and abrogates the Commandments, contradicts the very idea of Religion, as is evident from the derivation and meaning of the word. Religion comes from *religare*, to bind anew, and points to dogmas and duties, binding on the intelligence and conscience, and uniting us to God. The denial of free-will and of the obligation of the moral law, destroys the bond, and therefore annihilates the primary, fundamental, essential idea of Religion.

Protestantism, as it came from the hands of the first Reformers, deserves, also, to be branded as a Religion of blasphemy, for they made God the *author of sin*, and thereby evidently destroyed, on the one hand, the idea of sin, and, on the other, the idea of the infinite Sanctity of God. Here is the proof of my accusation.

Besides Luther's writings against Erasmus, to which I would refer you, I may quote Melanchthon, Luther's intimate disciple. In the following, Melanchthon faithfully expresses his master's opinions: " It is certain that all that happens, whether good or evil, comes from God. We assert, that God not only permits his creatures to act, but that He himself does every thing, so that as the vocation of Paul was the work of God, so was the adultery of David; and as the vocation of Paul was the work of God, so also was the treachery of Judas."*

* Martin. Chemnitz, Loc. Theol. p. 1, p. 173. Leyser, 1615.

Many others among Luther's adherents advocated the same opinion. Hence the Church in the Council of Trent framed the following canon against the Reformers: "If any one shall say, that it is not in the power of man to render his ways evil; but that God does the evil works, as He does the good, not only permissively, but properly and through Himself; so that the treason of Judas is God's own work, no less than the vocation of Paul; let him be anathema."*

Calvin, Zwingli, Beza, the three chief Swiss Reformers, are just as blasphemous in their doctrine as Melanchthon and Luther. Calvin makes use of such expressions as the following, not once only, but in a countless number o passages: "God impels man to do evil. He orders his fall, and for this purpose makes use of an interior inspiration in the heart of man."† Beza, the head of the Calvinists after Calvin's death, goes farther, and adds, "God creates a portion of men, only that He may use them as instruments to do evil."‡ By way of proving that this is not contrary to the justice and sanctity of God, Zwingli resorts to reasoning

* Conc. Trid, Sess. vi. can. vi.
† Calv. Instit. l. iv. c. xviii. § 2 l. iii. c. xxiii. § 8.
‡ Beza, Aphorism. xxii.

10

that would be laughable, were it not so shocking. He says, "God is above the law, therefore he cannot transgress the law, and consequently there is for Him no moral evil. He may do what He pleases. But the creature that commits evil by his impulse, sins, because God has given it a law." This Zwingli illustrates by a comparison worthy of the blasphemy. "A bull," he says, "may fill a whole herd of cattle with calves; this would only increase his merit, for he has no law. But, on the contrary, if his master should have more than one wife, he would be an adulterer, because a law has been given him, but the bull has none."* God and a bull! What a comparison! And still Zwingli goes on to explain by it that, though David's adultery was God's work, yet it was no sin in God who compelled him to commit it, but was a sin in David alone. I leave it to you to decide whether I have a right to call Protestantism a Religion of blasphemy.

You may say, What have we to do with Luther, Melanchthon, Calvin, Beza, or Zwingli? We do not agree with them. I grant it, but can you deny that you honor, as the authors of

* Zwingl. De Provid. cv. et vi.

the Reformation, the very authors of all this blasphemy? Is not the presumption against a Religion founded by such men? Must not such a Religion, at first sight, appear exceedingly suspicious, chiefly when you reflect on the commentary which the lives of the Reformers furnish to their teaching? Can you deny that they were passionate, and that Luther, Calvin, Zwingli, and their first followers publicly called each other wicked, mutineers, interpolators, reprobates, devils, and archdevils? Have you ever read any such thing of the Apostles and of the Fathers of the Catholic Church? Have you ever read that they loaded each other with insults, like those which Luther hurled against Henry VIII., and Henry VIII. in turn against Luther?

Such are the men from whom you have received your Religion. Their first unfortunate adherents would have done well to have asked them some higher proof of their mission than insult. At a later time, when some Protestant ministers came among the converts of St. Francis Xavier in India, after the death of that great Apostle, and exhorted them to become Protestants, those newly converted savages made this very striking and just reply, " As for your doctrines, we will not take the trouble to examine whether you are right or wrong; we are not learned enough for that; but we will propose an easy test that will at once clear up the whole matter. When the great Father [thus they called Xavier] came among us, he raised three dead men to life. If you wish us to change our faith for yours, you must first raise *six* dead men to life, that we may have more reason to believe you than him."

Your English forefathers would have done well to require a similar proof from the preachers of the new doctrines. They should have demanded from them, not only to raise six dead men to life, but to work twice as many miracles as had ever been wrought by all the Apostles and Saints of England, and by all the Apostolic men and Saints of the Catholic Church in the whole world, particularly as there was question of changing a Religion of consolation for a Religion of distress and despair, and the more so as this Religion was forced on them by the blood-stained hand of power.

Henry VIII. and Elizabeth, with their favorites and creatures, violently tore England from the Catholic Church. I have never read of their resuscitating the dead, but I have read of their murdering in cold blood hundreds of Priests and zealous Catholics, to introduce Protestantism into the country. These are historical facts. Your own writers have recorded them. Read the portrait of Henry and Elizabeth drawn by the famous Protestant Cobbett, in his "History of the Protestant Reformation in England and Ireland." He says of those two founders of the English Reformation, "Historians have been divided in opinion, as to which was the *worst man* that England ever produced, her father, [Henry VIII.] or Cranmer; but all mankind must agree, that this [Elizabeth] was the *worst woman* that ever existed in England, or in the whole world, Jezabel herself not excepted."*

Protestantism in its origin was by no means popular in England. It was introduced by tyrants, and forced on the nation by violence and bloodshed. It originated in the lust of Henry VIII. Indeed, Protestantism everywhere sprang from the two crimes which you most abhor, lust and despotism. It was originated in Germany by a lustful apostate monk; it was introduced in England by a lustful despotic monarch, who, after having written against Luther's Protestantism, ended by adopting it

---

* Cobbett, A History of the Prot. Reform., &c., Letter xi., No 348. See also Doellinger's celebrated History of the Reformation. See Bishop Spalding's History of the Reformation.

himself in order to satisfy his own adulterous desires, and because he wished to be his own pope, as the Pope of Rome refused to sanction his crime. The despotic work begun by Henry, was completed by a lustful, tyrannical Queen, his daughter. There is nothing better authenticated in all history than these startling facts, that Protestantism came from licentious apostate priests and monks, and from despotic, licentious sovereigns, not from the people. The origin alone of Protestantism renders it in the highest degree suspicious.

Protestantism is so far from having originated with the people or being the palladium of their liberties, that it was grasped at by monarchs as an instrument of despotism. The aim of the first Protestant rulers was to unite in their own hands both the temporal and spiritual powers, to enslave the souls as well as the bodies of the people, and be checked by no one. Wherever Protestantism failed to introduce despotism, it was owing in a great measure to the people, who turned against their sovereigns, and in some instances, by a just retribution, hurled them from their throne.

You are, then, Protestants to-day because English tyrants forced Protestantism on your ancestors. You have thrown off the political yoke of England, but you have not got rid of her religious influence. In a great measure, you remain Protestants because England remains Protestant. England's conversion to Catholic truth, could hardly fail to be followed by the conversion of the United States. You owe it to your love of truth and independence to determine your own course, and not to remain in Protestantism from mere education and habit.

CHAPTER II.

THE PRINCIPLE OF PROTESTANTISM.

I HAVE remarked above that one of the reasons why many among you remain Protestants, is the lack on their part of earnest examination. You neglect especially to investigate the principle of Protestantism, or the Protestant Rule of Faith.

The Catholic Rule of Faith is the infallible authority of the Church in matters of faith; the Protestant Rule is the Private Interpretation of the Bible. The Catholic believes whatever the Church teaches, because Christ has given her authority to teach in His name, and to teach infallibly what He has revealed. The Protestant professes to believe only what he can discover in the Bible by his own Private interpretation.

If you read the following pages with candor, without allowing yourselves to be swayed by prejudice, and with the determination to follow your convictions in the face of all obstacles whether from your family, your friends, or your worldly interests, it will be impossible for you to remain Protestants ; you will be fully convinced that the Catholic Church is the only true Church of Christ, and consequently that her infallible teaching is the true Rule of Faith ; that Protestantism, on the contrary, is not the true Church of Christ, and that its principle of Private Interpretation is absurd, and consequently that you cannot save your soul in Protestantism. The event shall prove whether you have the courage to examine for an hour with earnestness and candor.

SECTION I.

THE DIVINE TRUTH OF THE CATHOLIC CHURCH.—HER INFALLIBLE TEACHING.—THE TRUE RULE OF FAITH.

The whole controversy turns on this single question: What is the real motive alleged by the Reformers for separating from the Mother Church? It is reproached that the Catholic Church fell into error in the fifth or sixth century, lost her primitive form by innovations and abuses, and ceased to be the true Church of Christ. With this assertion Protestantism must stand or fall. The question is not whether Tetzel and Leo X. were good or wicked Catholics, the question is about the Church alone. *Has the Catholic Church, which was unquestionably the first Church, the one instituted by Christ, changed or has she not?* This is the whole question. Has she changed, no matter at what time, and could she change? The authors of Protestantism attempted to reform the Church as such, *the Church as a Church,* or else they could have no right to separate from her. The Church as a Church, according to them, had ceased to be the true Church.

To this fundamental supposition, which is the essential support of Protestantism, I oppose the following assertion: As long as reason remains reason, and Christ remains Christ, there can never, by any possibility, arise a deterioration in a Church Divinely instituted, and consequently there can never arise any occasion for a Reformation, nor any lawful reason for seceding from her.

I say, while reason remains reason there can never be even a possibility of deterioration in a Divinely constituted Church, and the bare thought of reforming such a Church is the greatest absurdity that can enter the human mind. This is clear from the following evident principle of reason: *Whatever God has ordained for an end must exist as long as the end exists, and no man, angel, or demon can change it.*

Here is an obvious illustration. God has created natural laws and powers in the visible world with a view to its existence, and no man, no angel, no demon can change them. Man may use or abuse the powers of nature, but change or reform them he cannot. What would you think of Luther and the rest of the Reformers, had they attempted to reform the sun, moon, and stars, and nature in general? To think of reforming the system of the world is madness: to think of reforming a Divinely instituted Church is absurdity and folly greater in an infinite degree.

The Church is a spiritual world, a universe formed by the power, and mercy, and grace of God. This creation is of an infinitely higher order than the material universe; it is more firmly fixed, more unchangeable, because it is founded for eternity. "Heaven and earth," says Christ, "shall pass away, but my words shall not pass away."* And again, "I say to thee, That thou art Peter, and upon this rock I will build my Church; and the gates of hell shall not prevail against it."† I do not inquire here what is meant by the rock, nor who is to be understood by Peter, but merely wish to direct your attention to the solemn, positive

* Matt., xxiv. 35.
† Ibid. xvi. 18.

assurance of Christ, that "the gates of hell shall not prevail against it."

This brings me to the second part of my assertion, that while Christ is Christ, that is, the Incarnate Son of God, His Church cannot change, because she is Divine, and has His promise to continue unchanged throughout all time. If you read the Scripture, you must know that all the promises of God, made by the prophets for a long series of centuries, had foretold that the Kingdom of Christ, His Church, would be eternal and unchangeable. The angel who announced the Incarnation likewise referred to this characteristic of the Church: "He shall reign in the house of Jacob forever, and of His kingdom there shall be no end."* But I will here confine myself to the promise of Christ above quoted. That promise is too clear and direct to be misunderstood, "The gates of hell shall not prevail against it." When Christ affirms so solemnly that the Church will not change, how can a Christian presume to say, The Church has changed? If the Church has changed, Christ is Christ no longer: He has not spoken the truth, and cannot be the Son of God. Then He has estab-

---
* Luke, i. 32, 33.

lished no Divine Church; men need not care whether they are Christians or Pagans; there is no essential difference between Protestants and Catholics, for both sides are deceived.

I wish every one of you would reflect on this argument as earnestly and with the same result, as an Englishman did, some years ago, in the Church of St. Peter's at Rome. He was a thorough and an obstinate Protestant. Like many of his countrymen, he had gone to Rome from curiosity. It was the Feast of the great Apostles St. Peter and St. Paul. The Pope, Pius VII., was to sing High Mass at St. Peter's. While the Pope, according to custom, was being carried through the Church, the choir sang the antiphon, " *Tu es Petrus,*—Thou art Peter, and on this rock I will build my Church, and the gates of hell shall not prevail against it." When the Englishman heard the words, " *Et portæ inferi non prævalebunt*—The gates of hell shall not prevail," he muttered to himself, " *Prævaluerunt*—They have prevailed." The choir repeated the words with greater force, " *Non prævalebunt;*" he repeated his "*prævaluerunt*—they have prevailed." But as if the power of the solemn chaunt had overwhelmed him, or as if he had suddenly heard the celestial choirs themselves, he paused; a sudden light had flashed upon him : the grace of God had illumined him; he had suddenly conceived the full significance of the promise of Christ the Son of God. For a while he was absorbed in reflection, and then striking the floor with his cane, he exclaimed aloud in a decided tone, "*Non praevalebunt*—They shall not prevail." He left the Church a convert to the Catholic faith.

A Febronian theologian employed by the famous Austrian Emperor Joseph II., was once so forcibly struck by those words of Christ, on hearing them read at Mass, that he was taken ill on the spot, so horrified was he at the thought of the crime he was committing in aiding the Emperor in his attacks on the rights of the Church. He understood that in spite of his impious efforts, the Church would continue as she was, and with her the Pope.

If you had heard Christ Himself address the promise to St. Peter alone of all the Apostles around him, you would have been deeply impressed with a sense of its infallible certainty. The promise is the same now as ever. If Christ is Christ, His promise is Divine ; it will be true to the end of the world, and the Church along with it, and no man, angel, or demon can corrupt or change her. If all the calumnies ever invented against Popes, Bishops, and Priests were true, you could not draw from them a shadow of conclusion against the Church. If every Pope, Bishop, and Priest had been a Judas, a Caiphas, a Pilate, a Herod, and an incarnate demon, all in one, not one of them, nor all of them together, could have vitiated the Church, for Christ has instituted her not for them alone, but for all men and for the salvation of men in all ages. The Church is not the work of men, any more than the world; therefore, they have as little power to corrupt one as to annihilate the other. They are free to use or to abuse the means of grace intrusted to the Church by her Founder, but they can no more alter the Church and its means of grace, than they can the course of the sun and moon. "Before you think of changing the Church," said St. Chrysostom in the fourth century, "change the sun, moon, and stars. Much sooner will you succeed in destroying the light of the sun, than in weakening the Church."

Hence I say, *The first Church is the true Church, or else there is no Divine Christian Church.* Americans, do you feel the irresistible power of this logical inference? Whoever does not pause to reflect upon it, cannot be in earnest to know the truth. In fact, either he does not believe Christ to be the Son of God and the Founder of a Divine Church, or he is incapable or unwilling to make a right use of his reason. Every one who believes Christ to be Christ, and consults his reason candidly, must hold this to be an evident principle, The Catholic Church, being the first Church, the Church instituted by Christ, is, and alone can be, the true Church of Christ.

This principle, in the present discussion, is to reason what the sun is to the universe. If a man closes his eyes against the sun, and complains that every thing is dark, you will not have recourse to astronomy to convince him that the sun and stars exist. So in the all-important question, Is the Catholic Church the true Church of Christ, and had the Reformers a just right to secede from her? I say the decision wholly depends on the question, Is the Catholic Church the only Christian Church reaching back to Christ? If the question is answered in the affirmative, then the Catholic Church is the true Church of Christ, the *Divine, unchangeable* Church; and it can never be lawful to separate from her, for the promise of Christ cannot change. Every one who will not hear the Church, that is, the Church instituted by Him, must " be held as the heathen and the publican."* Whatever she teaches as a Church must be true, or else she could change, which Christ has declared to be impossible: ' The gates of hell shall not prevail against it."

The irresistible force of this reasoning must be evident to every Protestant. If he does not become a Catholic, the reason must be sought in his heart, not in his mind. This is candidly acknowledged by a learned Protestant writer of our time, Gfroerer, in his " Critical Essay on Ancient Christianity." He thus expresses himself: " Catholic faith, if you admit its first principle, (that Christ is the Son of God, and His Church Divine, which no true Protestant can deny,) is as conclusive as the books of Euclid. There is no article of Catholic faith, which cannot be justified upon that principle."† Even Rousseau makes the following frank avowal : " Qu'on me prouve, qu'en matière de foi je suis obligé de me soumettre aux décisions de quelqu'un, dès demain je me fais Catholique et tout homme conséquent et vrai fera comme moi.‡—Let it be proved to me that, in matters of faith, I must submit to the decisions of any

---

* Matt., xviii. 17.
† Vol. 1., Preface, pp. 15–17.
‡ Rousseau, Lettre de la Montagne II.

one, and to-morrow I will become a Catholic, and every consistent and true man will do the same."

Rousseau is right in saying *every man*. As for the proof which he asks, it depends on the simple historical question, Which is the most ancient, or rather, the first Church, instituted by Christ Himself, the Son of God? I make the following supposition.

A man dies in 1862, leaving an only son born in 1830, to whom he has bequeathed all his property, and whose name, birthplace, and age, are all accurately described in the will. Two others come forward, each claiming to be the only son and universal heir of the deceased. The matter is brought before the court. As it is clearly proved that the deceased had only one son, all the judge has to do is to find out the birthplace, age, and name of each of the claimants. On interrogating two of them, he finds that the age of one is fifteen, and of the other twenty, and the birthplace and name of both different from those mentioned in the will. The third claimant proves by authentic documents, and by the testimony of the whole neighborhood, that his age, name, and birthplace perfectly agree with the description in the will. No other claimants appear. Indeed, the case is so clear that a child ten years old could decide it, and it is ridiculous to bring it before the court. The true son must be thirty-two years old, and every other claimant is an impostor.

The application to the Church is obvious. Let us take a non-Christian, for example a Turk, as judge, and he will decide, without difficulty, which of the three great Christian families are the true Christians, the Catholic, the Protestant, or the Greek and Oriental schismatic.

The Turk interrogates each of the three claimants: Do you sincerely believe that Christ was the true Son of God, and spoke the infallible truth? All answer, We sincerely believe so. Do you believe that Christ said, My Church shall never fail, or, The gates of hell shall not prevail against it? All answer, We believe so. Do you believe that the Apostles of Christ gave to His Church the name of Catholic? We do. When did Christ make that promise, establish His Church, and send forth His Apostles to announce it? Eighteen hundred years ago.

Now tell me, Protestants, how long have you existed? Three hundred years. Then, if four hundred years ago, a man wanted to become a

Protestant, where was he to apply? Protestantism was not yet in existence. What were your forefathers for fifteen hundred years? They were Catholics.

Tell me, schismatic Greeks and Orientals, how long have you existed? Eight hundred years. What is your name? Orthodox. What were your forefathers for a thousand years? Catholics.

And you, Catholics, how long have you existed? Eighteen hundred years. Where were you born? At Jerusalem. Who first called you Catholics? The Apostles. Who calls you so now? The whole world has called us Catholics for eighteen hundred years. How do you prove your age and your name? The history of the world, the testimony of all generations and of all races of men for eighteen hundred years prove it, and particularly the uninterrupted line of the successors of St. Peter,—Pius IX., Gregory XVI., Pius VIII., Leo XII., Pius VII., Pius VI., Clement XIV., and so on, back to Popes Clement, Linus, and Peter.

The Turk's decision cannot be doubtful. If Christ instituted only one Church, and that eighteen hundred years ago; if no Christian congregation but the Catholic, can prove that it has existed eighteen hundred years, or borne the name of Catholic given to the Church by the Apostles; if the Catholic alone has the true age, and bears the true name, then he must decide that the Catholics alone are the true Christians.

The Jew, in the well-known anecdote, gave a similar answer. Being asked by a Protestant and a Catholic, which of the two in his opinion was a member of the true Church, he answered, If Christ is not the Messiah, then we Jews are the only members of the true Church; if Christ is the Messiah, then the Catholics are; but as for you Protestants, you can never be members of the true Church. You have come too late for that.

When I was in Cincinnati, some years ago, a Methodist lady, whose daughter had lately become a Catholic, wished to see St. Philomena's church. The walls and ceiling of that church had been decorated with paintings. Standing before a large picture of the Blessed Virgin, she remarked to me, "We Methodists do not adore the Virgin Mary." "Neither do we," I replied, "but tell me, do you believe that the Virgin Mary was a Methodist?" "No, indeed." "Well," I said, "for my part, I should be unwilling to belong to a Religion which was not professed by the Mother of Christ."

Dr. Pusey and the Puseyites, in our time, have felt the truth of this axiom, *The first Church is the true Church, or there is no Church.* Hence they call themselves English Catholics. But it is as true now as in the age of St. Austin, that, " whether heretics like it or not, the whole world gives the name of Catholic to the Roman Catholic Church alone, and to no sect, even if the sects had a mind to claim the title."

This I have experienced in America. In 1852, at Manytowak, Wisconsin, I noticed a large and elegant church with a beautiful cross on its steeple, and remarked to an American lawyer, " I am astonished to find here so large a Catholic Church. Are there so many Catholics in this place?" " No, sir," he replied, " you are mistaken; it is a Puseyite church. The Puseyites call themselves Catholics. Some time ago the pastor of that church was at my house, and remarked to me, We, too, are Catholics, not Roman Catholics however, but English Catholics. I told him they were not the right sort of Catholics, but *counterfeit*." The lawyer's remark was certainly apposite.

Last year, in Philadelphia, on seeing a

Church with a beautiful cross, and asking whether it was a Catholic church, I was told it was not, but that the congregation called themselves Apostolic Catholics. "How Apostolic Catholics?" I asked. "If they can prove their right to the name, I will be one of their number this very day. But they cannot prove it. History shows too clearly that the Roman Catholic Church alone has descended from the Apostles, and in her alone is found the successor of St. Peter, in the person of the Pope and therefore she alone is the true Catholic Church. Hence she is the only true Church of Christ, and can be easily distinguished from all other churches, by simply applying the test of St. Ambrose, "Where Peter is, there is the Church."

Show me that St. Peter and his first successors were Protestants; prove that the earliest Catholics of England had Protestant parents; that England was Protestant for fifteen hundred years, and that the first Catholic in England was an apostate from Protestantism, and I will at once become a Protestant. Can you prove that? You cannot, were you to argue for all eternity. But if, on the other hand, it is clear as day that England was Catholic for fifteen hundred years; that the first Protestant on earth was an apostate Catholic priest and monk, who had said Mass and heard Confessions for many years; if it is true that his most powerful follower in England was an apostate Catholic King, and that all the original Protestants in England had Catholic parents, then I say, that living and dying I will remain a Catholic.

I am convinced that, if you believe in Jesus Christ and His promises, you must feel the invincible force of this argument, that the Catholic Church is the true Church, because she is the first Church; and that Protestantism is a counterfeit of Christianity, because it has not been instituted by Christ, nor has it descended from His Apostles: it is, and always will and must be, a mere deviation from the truth, an innovation introduced by a sensual, apostate monk, and a despotic, adulterous King.

A Catholic, living among Protestants, was once asked, whether he was not afraid of being buried in the Protestant graveyard. He replied, "No, gentlemen. Only dig a little deeper, and you will find nothing but Catholic bones." Americans, go to England, dig in the graveyards around the churches of your mother country, and under the dust of recent Protestant generations you will only find the ashes of your Catholic forefathers. Standing by those graves in the deep earnestness of thought with which death and eternity inspire every man who cares for his immortal hopes, reflect again and again upon the irresistible force of this proposition, The Catholic Church, being the first Church, is the true Church, or else there is no Divine Christian Church.

If you do not wish to be Catholics, you must become infidels, in order to retain a shadow of consistency—for the consistency of infidels, as I shall prove below, is nothing more than a shadow. But if you are determined to be Christians, and to believe as heretofore that Christ is Christ, and still persist in denying the truth of the Catholic Church, you do not, you cannot, retain even the shadow of consistency. Protestantism, in the light of revelation, history, and sound reason, in the very first step of our examination, appears most glaringly and utterly inconsistent.

OTHER MARKS OF THE DIVINITY OF THE CATHOLIC CHURCH.

Besides the unanswerable proof that the Catholic Church is the true Church, because she is the first Church, or the Apostolic Church, there are other proofs, no less evident, of her truth. The Church of Christ had been foretold under the image of " a mountain on the top of mountains, to which all nations should flow."* Christ compares her to a city built upon a mountain. The true Church of Christ must be visible. Instituted for the salvation of men in all time, she must have visible marks, by which she can be distinguished, in all ages and countries, from every sect and schism.

I will show that, besides the mark of apostolicity, of which I have just spoken, the Church of Christ must necessarily possess the characteristics of unity, sanctity, universality, and indestructibility; that these characteristics belong to the Catholic Church, and are completely wanting in Protestantism. Their presence in the Catholic Church casts upon her the vivid light of truth, and clearly shows her to be the true City of God; their absence in Protestantism leaves upon it the palpable darkness of error and exhibits it as an edifice of falsehood, a pure deformation of the truth.

* Isa., ii. 2.

UNITY.

The true Church of Christ must be one in her founder, for her founder must be Christ. She must likewise be one in faith, one in her means of salvation, one in government, and her unity must be visible. All this is evident from the Gospels and Epistles, and the Acts of the Apostles.

In regard to the unity of faith, it is evident that when Christ sent His Apostles " to teach all nations," He did not send them to teach contradictory doctrines. He commands all men to believe the faith preached by the Apostles, for he says, " He that believeth not shall be condemned."* He requires the same unity in the duties to be fulfilled by Christians, for He says, "Go ye, and teach all nations . . teaching them to observe all things whatsoever I have commanded you."† The promise of salvation is attached to the faith, hope, and charity which He has taught mankind, and to no other; He prayed to His heavenly Father,

---

* Mark, xvi. 16.
† Matt., xxviii. 19, 20.

"that they might all be one, as the Father is one in Him, and He in the Father."*

Unity of government is a no less necessary and undeniable characteristic of the true Church of Christ, as is evident both from the manner in which He sent His Apostles and from the power which he gave them: "As the Father hath sent me, I also send you."† "If he will not hear the Church, let him be to thee as the heathen and the publican."‡ Christ has made the characteristic of unity still more evident by the institution of a visible Head in the person of St. Peter, to whom He said in presence of all His Apostles, "I will give to thee the keys of the Kingdom of Heaven,"§ and later, in presence of several of His disciples, "Feed my lambs. Feed my sheep."‖

The Apostles, the inspired interpreters of the will of Christ, insist on the characteristic of unity as of absolute necessity to the Church of Christ. "One Lord, one Faith,"¶ says St. Paul, and he returns to the same point in his

---

* John, xvii. 21.
† John, xx. 21.
‡ Matt., xviii. 17.
§ Matt., xvi. 19.
‖ John, xx. 16, 17
¶ Ephes., iv. 5.

Epistles to the Philippians,* Galatians,† Romans,‡ and Corinthians.§ St Paul likewise dwells on the necessity of unity in the means of salvation: "The chalice of benediction which we bless, is it not the communion of the blood of Christ? And the bread which we break, is it not the partaking of the body of the Lord? For we being many, are one bread, one body, all who partake of one bread."‖ In regard to unity of government, you well know that St. Paul frequently refers to it, particularly in his Epistles to Timothy and Titus. The Acts of the Apostles, in describing the first council of Jerusalem, bear clear testimony that the head of the Church was Peter.

Wherever Christ speaks of the Church, He speaks of her as one Church. Indeed, since He is God, He cannot have founded conflicting Churches. All the figures under which Christ and His Apostles represent the Church, combine to demonstrate her absolute unity; a building, an inheritance, a flock, a kingdom, a city, an army, a body, and other figures made use of in reference to the Church, both in

* Philipp., ii. 2.
† Galat., i. 6-9.
‡ Rom., xvi. 17.
§ 1 Cor., i. 10.
‖ 1 Cor., x. 16, 17.

the Gospels and the Epistles, are all striking emblems of unity.

The absolute unity of the Church of Christ, as is evident from history, was universally acknowledged and invariably vindicated from the beginning, and throughout all the early ages of her existence, as well as in our own time. Every sect and schism that ever rose was uniformly cut off from her communion, because held to be incompatible with her unity.

The true Church of Christ must be one; contradictory doctrines cannot be all true; they cannot have been taught by Christ, nor belong to the Church which He founded.

It is scarcely necessary to prove that the unity of the Church must be a visible unity, for the Church is necessarily made up of visible men; those who are "to teach all nations to the end of time" must be visible; the bonds of communion established by Christ, the Sacraments, the Primacy of Peter, are visible; the figures of the Church are all drawn from visible objects, such as a city placed upon a mountain, a nation, a flock, an army. The Church must be visible, for Christ established her as a means of salvation for all men in all ages: an invisible Church would be useless as a means of salvation, for no man could discover her; no man could possibly avail himself of the means of salvation for the sake of which the Church was established.

That the Catholic Church possesses the characteristic of unity in faith, communion, government, and possesses it visibly, and in the highest perfection, is too clear to need lengthened demonstration. No man on earth can assign for her any other founder than our Lord Jesus Christ. No man on earth can name a single article of her faith, which is not equally professed by every Catholic in the whole world. No man can deny that she administers the same Sacraments over the whole globe, and offers the same Sacrifice from the rising to the setting sun. No one will affirm that Catholics, in any portion of the world, recognize any supreme visible Head in spiritual matters, but the successor of St. Peter, the Roman Pontiff. The unity of the Catholic Church is visible, and known to all the world.

On the other hand, Americans, you need only cast a glance at Protestantism to see its absolute want of unity. It is torn up by an enormous multiplicity of conflicting fragmentary sects, retaining not the least semblance of union. Even in the lifetime of Luther, as I observed above, Protestantism was split up into so many discordant churches, as to provoke Luther to the confession that the irremediable discord of Protestant sects stamped Protestantism visibly with the seal of error and falsehood.

Every one has heard of Bossuet's great "History of the Variations of Protestantism," and may read in that work the authentic proofs of its innumerable changes. Indeed, Protestantism, more changeable in its colors than the chameleon, more variable in its metamorphoses than fabled Proteus, is the strangest phenomenon of mutability that has ever appeared in the world.

Hœnighaus, a learned German author, compiled a complete Catholic Theology, from Protestant authors alone; not that he found in any of them a consistent body of Catholic doctrine, but by collecting the fragments of Catholic truth scattered through their disconnected systems, and reuniting them like the pieces of a broken mirror. Nothing more is required to show that Protestantism is only a departure from Catholic truth;—that, like a prodigal child, it has gone from its home, and squandered the venerable patrimony of the ancient holy Faith.

Some thirty years ago, the Duke of Anhalt Koethen, on his return from Paris, where he had become a Catholic, assembled his council of State and a number of Protestant pastors, in order to give them an account of his conversion. He told them that it was chiefly the consistent unity of the Catholic doctrine, that had induced him to examine it, and finally brought about his conversion. He had been unable to discover any unity among Protestants. The pastors contended that the accusation was unfounded; that Protestants agreed in the essential points. The Duke asked them, "Do you hold the doctrine of justification as an essential point of faith?" "We do." "Well, then," continued the Duke, turning to one of the pastors, " please tell me how you define that doctrine." The pastor gave his definition, but had hardly done so when another pastor exclaimed, " Excuse me, Duke, that is not my idea of justification, I understand it quite differently." A third one followed with a different definition. The Duke ended the dispute, by remarking, " Gentlemen, you have just given me a proof of Protestant unity." You cannot say that Catholics contradict each other in that manner. In matters of opinion they may and do differ, but not in matters of faith. The moment a Catholic denies an article of faith, were he an Aquinas in learning, he ceases to be a Catholic. A Protestant who contradicts your religious ideas, remains a Protestant, and is free to maintain his views against all Protestants, for your Religion gives every man an absolute right to be his own judge in questions of faith.

SANCTITY

Is the second necessary characteristic of the true Church of Christ. It is evident that the Church of Christ must be holy in her founder, for her founder is Christ Himself. Her means of salvation must be holy, for Christ established her to be a means of sanctification forever. " For them do I sanctify myself, that they also may be sanctified in truth," etc.* " Be you perfect as your heavenly Father is perfect."†

The language and spirit of the apostolic Epistles, their precepts, institutions, admonitions, counsels, all demonstrate that the true Church of Christ must be holy, and an evident

* John, xvii. 19 et seqq.
† Matt., v. 48.

means of holiness. "Christ loved the Church and delivered Himself up for it, that He might sanctify it, cleansing it by the laver of water in the word of life; that He might present it to Himself a glorious Church, not having spot or wrinkle, nor any such thing; but that it should be holy and without blemish."*.

History testifies that the Church of Christ, in the primitive ages, possessed the character of sanctity, and therefore she must possess it always, for, as I have shown, the Church of Christ cannot change. The Fathers and early pastors of the Church labored night and day, by word and writing, to sanctify the faithful, and only recognized those as living members of the Church, whose lives were truly Christian.

The Catholic Church clearly possesses the character of sanctity. Her doctrine, her Sacraments, her Sacrifice are holy, and are means of holiness. Saints, whose heroic virtue God has attested by manifest miracles, are claimed by the Catholic Church alone, and belong to her alone. To be alone the mother of all the Saints, of all the heroes of Christianity, whose purity of life is the light and admiration of the

---

* Ephes., v. 25-27.

world, is an imposing mark of the truth of the Catholic Church.

In the first rank of her Saints, as I mentioned in another point of view, appear seventeen millions of martyrs, of every age, sex, rank, and condition of life, all of whom died for the truth of the Catholic faith. This was during the first three centuries of the Catholic Church. What was so magnificently begun, has continued in every age down to our own day. Witness Japan, China, Tartary, Africa, America in the last two centuries. Witness the soil of our own United States, reddened with the blood and sanctified by the ashes of the Missionaries who fell under the Indian tomahawk, or were consumed at the Indian stake. Witness China, Cochin-China, Tonquin, and Corea, in the last fifty years, and Syria at this very time.

Next in rank to these martyred heroes of the Cross, is the venerable line of the holy Fathers and Doctors of the Church, from Hermas, Clement, Justin, in the first centuries, down to St. Bernard, in the twelfth, all of whom were Catholics.

Along with them, in every age, there is a host of other Saints, all witnesses to the truth of the Catholic Church. Beginning with St.

Peter and Linus, his first successor, we have a countless number of holy Popes, Bishops, men of learning and eminence, heroic Confessors of the faith in every condition and grade of society.

These are the true nobility, the flower of our race: their genuine greatness of virtue is admired even by our enemies. Leibnitz, one of the most learned Protestants of his age, confesses, in his System of Theology, that the Catholic Church has every reason to point to the heroic virtues of her Saints, in proof of her high birth as the Church of Christ.

Ignorant men, and even persons otherwise well-informed, but prejudiced against the Church, may question the miracles by which God has attested the heroic virtues and the glory of our Saints; but no one can question the eminence of their virtues. No one can question their astonishing actions, their zeal, their labors, their sacrifices for the conversion of nations and the relief of suffering; and this, after all, is the main point.

But as for the miracles themselves, they are not so easily got rid of as some of you may imagine. It is not so easy to throw a reasonable doubt on them. You cannot name another tribunal that performs its duties with so much impartiality, caution, and severity, as the Roman *Rota*, the court in which the merits of reputed saints, and the miracles wrought after their death, are discussed and decided on. This undeniable fact it is worth while to illustrate at some length.

When application is made for the canonization of a reputed saint, no step is taken by the Roman tribunal, until evident proofs are brought forward upon oath, that the person in question practised, in life and death, not only eminent theological and moral virtues, but heroic virtues tested by extraordinary trials.

No miracles are admitted in proof of sanctity, except such as were wrought after the death of the servant of God in favor of persons who had recourse to his intercession. No miracles performed during his lifetime, were they hundreds or thousands in number, as in the case of St. Gregory Thaumaturgus or St. Francis de Hieronymo, are admitted or even examined with a view to canonization. As to miracles wrought after death, Rome requires that they be first ascertained, in a judicial process, by the Bishop of the Diocese where they are said to have occurred, and testified to by creditable witnesses under oath. If the Bishop rejects he miracles, no further step is taken by the

Roman court. If he admits them as genuine, Rome is not yet satisfied, but appoints another judicial commission to renew the investigation and the witnesses summoned are again examined under oath. If both commissions agree in declaring the miracles undeniably genuine, a third process is instituted before the Roman *Rota:* all the facts are re-examined, the value of the testimony subjected to a rigorous discussion, and the case decided only after mature and protracted deliberation. Indeed, the slowness of the Roman court is proverbial.

A recent event will illustrate it. An Englishman at Rome, in a conversation with a Cardinal on the truth of the Catholic Religion, expressed the opinion that Catholic Saints are made at pleasure, and miracles forged to support the canonization. The process of the canonization of St. Francis Regis was then pending. " Sir," replied the Cardinal, " the best answer I can give you, is to let you examine for yourself the pieces in a process of canonization actually going on. Read these papers." The papers were the juridical record of some hundreds of miracles wrought by the intercession of St. Francis Regis after his death. The Englishman was astonished at the accuracy of investigation displayed in the record, and at the weight of testimony by which every miracle was supported. On returning the papers to the Cardinal, he could not help expressing his astonishment. "If every Roman miracle," he observed, "were proved as well as these, I should have no difficulty in believing all the miracles we read of in the lives of your Saints." "Why sir," answered the Cardinal, smiling, "the Roman court is not satisfied with the proofs of a single one of those miracles."

Now tell me, my Protestant friends, how many Saints Protestantism has produced; give me their names, and let me know what miracles have been performed by their prayers, in their lifetime or after their death.

The lives of your founders are notorious all the world over. You would be ashamed to read Luther's Table Talk before your children. But not to enlarge on the sensual German Reformer, I will invite you only to look back to the country from which you have received the Reformation. Will you appeal to the adulterer Henry VIII; or to the *Virgin* Queen of more than suspicious memory? How many Protestant martyrs, bishops, pastors, widows, virgins are set down in your Calendar of Saints? What miracles have they performed? You are so far from claiming any Saints of your own, that the questions must appear ridiculous. Still, in the Apostles' Creed, you say with us, "I believe in the communion of Saints," and confess your belief in "the *holy* Catholi Church." The Church, such as you have made it for yourselves, is a withered tree bearing no fruits of sanctity.

The very names you receive at your birth must remind you of the absolute barrenness of Protestantism. You have not a single Protestant Saint. If you wish to give your children a Christian name, the name of a Saint, you are obliged to have recourse to the Catholic calendar. You call your children by Catholic names, such as Charles, Francis, Henry, Edward, Catharine, Elizabeth. You even give them the names of Catholic Saints who lived after the Reformation,—Aloysius, Teresa, etc. Those among you who dislike all such names, because they would remind them too often of the Catholic Church as the Mother of Saints, have to go back to the old Jews, and borrow the names of Abraham, Isaac, Jacob, David, Reuben, Rebecca, Sarah, Judith, etc.; or descend to a lower level, and adopt names from among the saints of the political tribune.

You know as well as I do what has come to

be the ideal of sanctity with many who call themselves Protestants. When they can say of a man, He is a perfect gentleman, or of a woman, She is an accomplished lady, they are satisfied. When a man outstrips his neighbo in business, and gets rich in a short time, he is raised on the altars of public admiration. This language may sound harsh and bitter, yet every one of you will say, It is so. Confessing, as you do in the Creed, that the Church is holy, and still not to be able to show a single Saint, is bad enough.

UNIVERSALITY

Is the third necessary character of the Church of Christ. He founded His Church for all times and all places. " Go ye and teach all nations. . . . And behold I am with you all days even to the consummation of the world."* " I will ask the Father, and He shall give you another Paraclete, that He may abide with you forever."†

Hence the rapid spread of the Church in the

* Matt., xxviii. 20.
† John, xiv. 16.

very first age of her existence. The Acts of the Apostles, the Epistles of St. Paul,* and all cotemporary history, testify to her diffusion over the whole Roman empire, and beyond its boundaries, within the lifetime of the Apostles.

It is self-evident, indeed, that if Christ founded any Church at all, it must have been for the whole human race, because the wants of men, which He designed His Church to supply, are substantially the same in all men and in all ages.

The characteristic of universality evidently belongs to the Catholic Church. She is universal in time and place. She exists in all the nations and regions of the globe; she counts her ages by the ages of Christianity; the whole world is her home, and all time her duration. She is universal, particularly, in the sense that she is the Mother of all the races and tribes ever converted to Christianity.

What Tertullian remarked of the heretics of his time, sixteen hundred years ago, is true to-day, " They can pervert, but not convert, that is of Catholics they make non-Catholics; of children of one Church, sectarians and schismatics; of Christians, non-Christians; of believers, infidels: but to convert one nation of

---

* Rom., i. 8.; Coloss. i. 5, 6

heathens to Christianity is beyond their power. Such is the loud testimony of history in favor of the Catholic Church."

Every nation, that is Christian now, or ever was Christian, was converted by Catholic missionaries. Let us go through the list, beginning at the extreme west of Europe. St. Patrick and his companions, all Catholics, converted Ireland. St. Augustine, a Catholic, and his Catholic companions converted England. France was converted by St. Remigius and his Catholic fellow-bishops; Germany by St. Boniface, St. Kilian, Willibald, and others, all Catholics; Denmark, Sweden, and Norway, by Ansgar and Sturmius, two Catholic bishops; Prussia, by St. Adalbert, a Catholic; Sclavonia and Bulgaria, by Cyril and Methodius, two Catholic bishops; Russia, by Ignatius of Constantinople and his associates, all Catholics. St. Stephen, a Catholic king, converted Hungary through Catholic missionaries. In Asia, from Japan, China, and India, to the Mediterranean; in Africa, from ocean to ocean, every nation and tribe converted to Christianity, was converted by Catholic missionaries. On the Western Continent, since its discovery by Catholic navigators, it has been the same. The savages of Peru, Chili, Brazil, Buenos

Ayres, Paraguay, the whole of South America, as far as it is Christian, has been evangelized and converted by the Catholic Church. Catholics have converted and civilized many tribes of Indians in Central America and Mexico. In North America, your own historians have recorded the labors of Catholic missionaries in every wood, desert, and prairie. The Christian tribes north of the Lakes and in several other parts of Canada, in Oregon, and Kansas, are the fruits of Catholic zeal; and but for the outbreak and interference of Protestantism, our success would have been much greater. Catholic missionaries, observes Dr. Brownson, in a number of his celebrated Quarterly, have converted and civilized numerous Indian tribes in North America, and still more of them in South America. You could drive them before you, but you could not convert them. The islands of the Pacific, at this moment, are evangelized with great success by hosts of intrepid Catholic missionaries.

Name, if you can, a single heathen nation converted by Protestants. No such nation exists. I know you have expended millions of money in keeping up large families of missionaries, and scattering millions of Bibles on every shore to which your vessels sail. But your

Bible missions cannot convert the heathen. The savage and the Chinese use your Bibles to light the calumet or the opium bowl. The reports of your own interested and richly paid missionaries, furnish sufficient ground for doubting your success. It is certain that St. Francis Xavier alone, in ten years, converted a thousand times more Pagans in India and Japan, than you have done, with all your Bible and Missionary Aid Societies, in three hundred years. The missionary success of a single Catholic institution, the Roman Propaganda, surpasses, beyond comparison, the combined result of the influence, wealth, and power of Great Britain and America.

INDESTRUCTIBILITY

Is the fourth necessary character of the Church of Christ, to which I propose to direct your attention. "I say to thee, That thou art Peter, and upon this rock I will build my Church; and the gates of hell shall not prevail against it." "Go ye, and teach all nations... Behold I am with you all days, even to the consummation of the world."* From these and similar passages before cited, it is evident, that Christ will never suffer His Church to be destroyed.

Hence, in the earliest times, indestructibility was held to be an essential characteristic of the Church of Christ. St. Jerome, in the fourth century, wrote, "The Church is built on Peter. No storm can shake her, no raging tempest overthrow her."† St. Alexander, Bishop of Alexandria in the beginning of the same age, wrote to Alexander of Constantinople, "We acknowledge but one Church, the Catholic and Apostolic, which, as she never can be vanquished, though the whole world should assail her, so, on the other hand, conquers and destroys every atrocious attack of heresy." Indeed, if the Church could be destroyed, Christ would have failed in the object he had in view in founding her, which was to make her a means of salvation for all ages. That Christ has failed in this design no one will say.

Now, the Catholic Church alone on earth possesses the character of indestructibility Everything on earth decays, except the Catho-

---
* See texts, *ut supra.*
† Comment. in cap. xvi Matt.

lic Church. She is the image of her Founder, the most perfect reflection in the world of the immutability of God, of that supreme Beauty, which St. Augustine called ever ancient and ever new. Like Christ her Founder, she is " yesterday and to-day, and the same forever." Like St. John, the disciple whom Jesus loved, the Church, the Spouse of Jesus, rises out of persecution with new vigor and renewed youth.

You call her the Old Church. She is old, but as youthful in her old age, as when she went forth on Pentecost, fresh from the hands of the Holy Ghost, to the conquest of the world. Name a Church or sect in our age that equals her in vigor. You know the words of Gamaliel, the Pharisee, in the Acts: "If this design, or work, be of men, it will fall to nothing; but if it be of God, you are not able to destroy it: lest perhaps ye be found to oppose God."* What would Gamaliel say at this hour, were he to rise from the dead? Nearly nineteen hundred years have since gone by, nineteen centuries of struggles and of triumph. Power, learning, genius, heresy, schism, vice, determined foes without, envenomed conspirators within, all earth and hell

---

* Acts, v. 38, 39.

combined, have been laboring for nineteen centuries at her destruction, and the Church survives in her pristine vigor.

The world has not seen any other example of such a duration. St. Augustine said of the rapid spread of Christianity, that by itself alone it was a sufficient proof of the Divinity of the Catholic Church. The dilemma he made use of, is just as unanswerable when applied to the duration of the Catholic Church. Either the Catholic Church has existed for nineteen centuries by a miracle, or without a miracle: if by miracle, she is Divine; if without miracle, in spite of atrocious and ever-enduring opposition, on the ruins of all the empires that ever rose or flourished around her, then she herself is the greatest of all miracles, and you have the highest of all proofs that she is Divine.

History presents no parallel to her insignificant beginning, rapid growth, and permanent duration. At the moment when Peter came from Antioch to Rome, and entered the Imperial City, a poor, barefoot, way-worn traveler covered with dust, if a prophet standing at the gate had pointed him out with outstretched arm, and said to the passing throng, "Do you see that gray-haired stranger? He is a poor fisherman from Galilee. The successors of that Jewish fisherman will rule the world to its utmost boundaries from your own City and on the ruins of your Empire; kings, princes, nations, republics, the Roman, Greek, and barbarian, will acknowledge their religious sway, and obey their spiritual commands for centuries after the Roman power shall have departed forever, and the remembrance of your glory hardly survive in the memories of the remotest posterity." Every Roman would have laughed at the prophecy, and pointed at the prophet as a madman; and when, not many years later, Peter was nailed on a cross with his head downwards, they might have brought the prophet to the spot, and said in scorn, There hangs your prophecy. And yet upon that very spot, reddened with the blood of the Prince of the Apostles, and known under the name of the Confession of St. Peter, has sprung up the mighty tree that now overshadows the earth, its trunk rooted at Rome in the martyred ashes of the first Pope, growing more vigorous with every storm that assails it, its branches still spreading and growing mightier, as ages multiply upon its venerable head, and the nations that seek shelter in its holy shade become more numerous from age to age.

Religious, Catholic Rome, said Leo the

Great, has become mightier than Pagan Rome in the meridian of her splendor. And what is particularly worthy of repeated notice, her unequalled duration and unrivalled religious sway have not been the work of human power all human power has opposed her. For nineteen hundred years the mighty hand of leagued envy and malice has been upon the Tree endeavoring to tear it up from the soil, and leave it a withered trunk to be despised and forgotten.

You know the fierce rage of the Roman Empire against the Catholic Church for three hundred years. After Constantine had placed the Cross upon his crown and upon the banners of his armies, a new race of persecutors arose, beginning with his son Constantius, and continuing through the Middle Ages down to our time: emperors, kings, consuls have hardly ever ceased to assail the Catholic Church with the cunning of a Julian or the violence of a Valens. The history passing before your own eyes, while I trace these lines, Turin, Paris, the midnight conspiracies at Rome, present scenes of consummate hatred, exquisite cunning, refined malice, bloodthirsty cruelty, that are not unworthy a Julian or a Diocletian.

Philosophy, heresy, schism, have united their

efforts with the attacks of power. From Celsus, under the first Cæsars, to Voltaire, Strauss, Saint-Simon, Fourier, Leroux, philosophy has exerted its evil genius to sap the foundations of Catholic dogmas. From Simon Magus and the Gnostics to Luther and the Mormons, from Photius to Febronius, heresy has not ceased to aim at the corruption of her faith, and schism at the destruction of her unity. Men have dug at the roots of the Tree, and sought to undermine it; they have tried to overthrow the venerable trunk, and have hacked at its branches. Still its roots are as firmly fixed as ever, the trunk stands upright, and growing still. If a branch has fallen, it lies withered where it fell, and another bough has replaced it. When England and a part of Germany fell off from the Church, Paraguay, Japan, India, the extreme East and West, rose in their stead. Earth and hell, passion and malice, have done their worst, and they have failed and shall forever fail.

Were the Pope and the Church to be driven back to the Catacombs from which they rose in triumph fifteen hundred years ago, the persecution would but prepare for them another triumph. Pius IX. knows it, and hence his fearless attitude, awing his enemies, and attracting the admiration of the world. The whole Catholic Church knows it, and hence the calm with which we look forward to the future. Come what may, the Church will stand. "The gates of hell shall not prevail against her." Christ is with us "to the consummation of the world."

Everywhere and in all times the Church conquers. Everywhere and in all times, she is the indestructible Kingdom of the Truth. She may be stripped and sent forth naked into the world, still she conquers, for she remains the dispenser of the graces of God to men, the guide of the human race, the hand that opens the gates of heaven, the only hope of salvation. "I will give to thee the keys of the kingdom of heaven."*

Now, turn to Protestantism, and compare it with the Church. The opposition between light and darkness is not more complete. The Catholic Church lives, Protestantism is dead. It is a branch fallen from the Tree, withered even in the time of him who cut it off, and hewn to fragments, its dry leaves long since reduced to dust and scattered to the four winds of heaven. The Protestantism of Luther, Calvin, Zwingli is destroyed. Hardly

* Matt. xvi. 19.

any one now-a-days believes as they believed. Even Baptism is fast being given up altogether. Many who bear the name of Protestants, are infidels in principle and practice: unbaptized, they do not possess the necessary qualification to be Christians. Unbaptized Protestants are more numerous in this country, than the baptized adherents of all the Protestant denominations put together.

Your meeting-houses would long since have been deserted, your sects reduced to mere names, but for your keeping up a semblance of life by your Revivals. The country, as far as it is Protestant, would no longer exhibit any sign of Christianity, were it not for your strict Sunday laws imposing an appearance of Christianity.

But all your Revivals and Sunday laws, never will and never can revive Protestantism. Protestants may continue to exist, but Protestantism is dead, and its death was almost coeval with its birth. A Protestantism, one and united, has no existence, if it ever had.

To conclude, the Catholic Church alone has the characteristics of the Church which Christ founded; she alone, therefore, is the true Church of Christ, and out of her pale there is no salvation. Every candid man who examines the question, can easily convince himself of it. The Catholic Church is the City of God, visible over the whole earth to every man of good will. Protestantism lacks every one of the characteristics of the true Church of Christ, and cannot lead to Heaven.

Study the history of Catholicity and that of Protestantism with the candor of the celebrated Swiss Protestant Hurter, and like him you will become convinced that Protestantism is nothing more than a deviation from the truth, and that the Catholic Church alone is the identical Church founded by Christ. As soon as a Protestant begins to look into the groundwork of his creed, his belief begins to waver. A Catholic is secure. History, reason, experience, studies of every kind, confirm him in his faith. A true Catholic meets martyrdom with the full assurance that he dies for the truth. Peter the Martyr, a convert to the Catholic faith from Manicheism, when he fell under the hatchets of the heretics, and could no longer profess his faith aloud, wrote in the sand with his blood— I believe. Every Catholic is as firmly convinced of the truth of his faith, as that hero was when about to appear before God.

THE INFALLIBILITY OF THE CATHOLIC CHURCH, THE RULE OF FAITH.

The Catholic Church is the true Church of Jesus Christ; therefore she is Infallible. No man of logical mind can dispute this consequence. The Infallibility of the Church follows evidently from her character as the Divinely commissioned Teacher of all nations to the end of time; and it is further confirmed by the express promises of Christ, and by the conduct of the primitive Church.

I say, in the first place, that the Infallibility of the Church is a necessary consequence of her Divine commission as the Teacher of men. To deny the Infallibility of the Church, while you admit her Divine commission, is to impeach the veracity and the wisdom of God.

Christ commanded His Church to teach all nations to the end of time: to pretend that His Church is fallible, is to assert implicitly that, in case she errs, He commanded her to teach falsehood, and made it obligatory on men to believe error. If Christ has not secured the Infallibility of the Church by the assistance of His Spirit, error must inevitably be taught as Divine truth, for the Church teaches in His name, and enforces her doctrines as derived from Him, and therefore as Divine truth. I repeat it, therefore, the character of the Church as a Divinely commissioned Teacher, is the proof of her Infallibility.

Secondly, her claim to Infallibility is confirmed by the clearest and most explicit promises of Christ. He affirmed that He would build His Church upon a rock, and that the gates of hell should not prevail against her. He addressed His Apostles in the following explicit language : " As the Father has sent me, I send you. Go ye, therefore, and teach all nations, teaching them to observe all things whatsoever I have commanded you. And behold, I am with you all days, even to the consummation of the world." " He who hears you, hears me." " And when the Paraclete, the Holy Ghost shall come, whom the Father shall send in my name, He will teach you all things, and bring all things to your mind whatsoever I shall have said to you." " I shall ask the Father that He may abide with you forever."

According to these promises, the Holy Ghost is to perform two great functions in the Church of Christ—first, "to teach her all things," secondly, to "bring all things to her mind" which Christ has taught her; and to do all this *forever*. What the Holy Ghost "teaches" the Church, must be the truth; that of which He reminds her, is the doctrine of Christ. The Church, therefore, has an infallible guide, who, because He is infallible, must render her infallible, and who, on all proper occasions, puts her in mind of "all things whatsoever" which Christ has taught her. Hence, in listening to the teaching of the Church, we listen to the voice of God. Whoever refuses to listen to her, is to be regarded "as a heathen and a publican."

I ask you, can you reflect on these distinct promises of Christ, without concluding that He endowed the Church with the attribute of Infallibility? Will you, while believing that Christ is God, take it amiss that we believe in His promises, or that we abhor the thought that His promises have failed, as they must have done if His Church has erred or can err? If the Church is fallible, she was not built upon a rock, but upon a quicksand, and the gates of hell may prevail against her: indeed, if we are to believe Protestantism, the gates of hell have long since prevailed against the Church of

Christ. But if the Church has erred, Christ cannot be God—He would be an impostor; the Holy Spirit is not, has not been with the Church of Christ; those who hear the Church, would often hear, not God, but the spirit of error; while those who refuse to recognize her Divine authority, would not be heathens and publicans, but wiser than believers. All this evidently involves, in the judgment of all who really believe in Christ as the Son of God, contradiction and blasphemy.

Thirdly, the claim of Infallibility is further confirmed by the manner in which the primitive Church fulfilled her Divine mission. On the day of Pentecost, immediately after the reception of the Holy Ghost, the Apostles began the ministry of teaching, committed to them by the Son of God. Later, we find them assembled again in Jerusalem in solemn council, prefacing their decisions with the following remarkable declaration: "It has seemed good to the Holy Ghost and to us," thus claiming the infallible assistance of the Spirit of God.

It must be remarked likewise, that, while the Apostles spread the Gospel amongst the nations, they selected and ordained proper persons to be their coadjutors and successors, just as they elected an Apostle to take the place of Judas Iscariot. They would not permit any one not ordained and sent by them o teach in the name of Christ. The faith taught by the Church must be Apostolic; that is, it must be the same now as it was in the time of the Apostles. This follows from the very nature of the Church of Christ, for, as I have shown, the Church cannot change; it follows from the promises of Christ, and it is strongly inculcated by His Apostles. A curse is pronounced against any one who should attempt to preach a new doctrine. "Though I, or an angel from heaven," says St. Paul, " preach any other gospel unto you, than that you have received, let him be accursed."* The Church, therefore, must be infallible now, as she was when Christ established her, for if she is fallible we cannot be certain that she teaches the same doctrine as the Apostles.

The Church is unchangeable; she is the same now as in the days of Christ. Are you prepared to say that the Church was fallible in the time of Christ and the Apostles? If she was infallible then, she is infallible now. The attribute of infallibility was not a prerogative

* Galat., i.

exclusively attached to the persons of the Apostles, but inseparably connected with their office, in the same manner as the Church was not instituted for them alone, but for the salvation of men to the end of time.

The Son of God was sent into the world by the Eternal Father, to create and organize the Church, and He sent forth the Apostles with the same supernatural power and perpetual authority that He Himself had received from the Father. "As my Father sent me, so I send you." The Apostles and their legitimate successors constitute one and the same Church "Behold I am with you all days even to the consummation of the world." The supernatural power which Christ communicated to His Church, was given for the preservation of the faith which He had revealed, and cannot be limited by time, any more than the faith itself. Like Christ Himself the Church is "to-day, and yesterday, and the same forever;" she is Infallible in all ages.

The argument which I have thus briefly stated is developed with great cogency and eloquence, in an essay by Dr. Brownson on the "Constitution and Organic Character of the Church;" from which I make the following extract:

"The Catholic Church, as a body or corporation, the only sense in which it is alleged to have any teaching faculty at all, is not an aggregation of individuals who at any time compose it—a body born and dying with them but the contemporary of our Lord and His Apostles, in immediate communion with them, and thus annihilating all distance of time and place between them and us. She is, in the sense supposed, a corporation, and, like every corporation, a collective individual possessing the attribute of immortality. She knows no interruption, no succession of moments, no lapse of years. Like the eternal God, who is ever with her, and whose organ she is, she has duration, but no succession. She can never grow old, never fall into the past. The individuals who compose her body may change, but she changes not; one by one they may pass off, and one by one be renewed, while she continues ever the same. . . . . The Church to-day is identically that very body which saw our Lord when he tabernacled in the flesh. She who is our dear Mother, and on whose words we hang with so much delight, beheld with her own eyes the stupendous miracles which were performed in Judea eighteen hundred years ago; she assisted at the preaching of the

Apostles on the day of Pentecost, when the Holy Ghost descended upon them in cloven tongues of fire; she heard St. Peter, the prince of the Apostles, relate how the Spirit descended upon Cornelius and his household, and declare how God had chosen that by his mouth the Gentiles should hear the Word of God and believe; she listened with charmed ear and ravished heart to the last admonition of the disciple whom Jesus loved :—' My dear children, love one another;' she saw the old temple razed to the ground, the legal rights of the old covenant abolished, and the once chosen people driven out from the Holy Land, and scattered over the earth; she beheld pagan Rome, in the pride and pomp of power, bled under her persecuting emperors, and finally planted the cross in triumph on her ruins. She has been the contemporary of eighteen hundred years, which she has arrested in their flight and made present to us, and will make present to all generations as they rise. With one hand she receives the *depositum* of faith from the Lord and his commissioned Apostles; with the other she imparts it to us.

" . . . What needs she, to do it with infallible certainty? Simply protection against forgetting, misunderstanding, and misstating;

and this she has, because she has our Lord always abiding with her, and the Paraclete, who leads her into all truth, and 'brings to her remembrance' all the words spoken to her by our Lord himself personally, or by his inspired Apostles,—keeping her memory always fresh, rendering her infallible assistance rightly to understand and accurately to express what she remembers to have been taught."

Consequently the Infallibility of the Church does not, as many Protestants imagine we teach, extend to every object of science or politics, but is exclusively confined to the teaching and preservation of that Divine faith which Jesus Christ revealed for the salvation of mankind In this respect, she demands our unconditional submission to her decisions, but only when she promulgates her doctrine by a solemn definition. In doing so she, as we have shown, only exercises her legitimate right. Her Infallible teaching is the only Rule of Faith.

I may remark in conclusion, that the practice of those who deny the Infallibility of the Church, is in contradiction with their theory. While asserting that there is no infallible authority in matters of faith, they have recourse invariably to some supreme and final authority which they practically hold to be infallible.

Whatever they assume as their Rule of Faith, whether reason, Scripture, common sense, private interpretation or private inspiration, they practically regard it as an authority from which there is no appeal, as an authority *infallible* in matters of faith. It is strange, indeed, that non-Catholics hardly ever perceive this striking inconsistency between their theory as regards the Church and their practice in deciding upon their own belief. In the following pages, you will find a further illustration of the inconsistency of Protestantism.

SECTION II.

THE UNTENABILITY OF THE PROTESTANT PRINCIPLE.

I have now developed the conclusive argument that the Catholic Church is the true Church because she is the first Church, and alone possesses the marks of the true Church of Christ, and that her infallible teaching is the Rule of Faith. What decisive reasons have you to convince yourselves, that what you believe is the true Religion of Christ? You appeal to the Bible.

That the Bible is the only Rule of Faith, is the fundamental doctrine of Protestantism, first asserted by Martin Luther. "What do I care," said Luther, "for six hundred Augustines and Jeromes? With the Bible in our hand, we can judge the Fathers, the Apostles, and even the Church.

The Bible is the war-cry of Protestantism. No doubt, the Bible is a Divinely inspired book, but the manner in which many among you appeal to the Bible, reminds me of the tumult raised at Ephesus by the preaching of St. Paul. The only answer which the Ephesians would give him, was to cry for two hours, " Great is Diana of the Ephesians." Many Protestants do no better. Instead of listening to our arguments, or trying to answer them, they cry out, The Bible, the Bible,—as if, indeed, Catholics denied the Bible. " When the town-clerk of Ephesus had appeased the people, he said, Ye men of Ephesus, what man is there that knoweth not that the city of Ephesus is a worshipper of the great Diana?" I would ask, likewise, Who is there among us that rejects the Bible? The Catholic Church has always taught, and Catholics have always believed, that the Bible is the word of God; they believed it fourteen centuries before the birth of Protestantism. I will show you, that as long as the Bible is the Bible, that is, the word of God, you can never justify Protestantism from the Bible.

But, before entering on the discussion, I ask you, From whom did you receive the Bible?

Was it written by Luther under Divine inspiration, or brought down to him from Heaven by an angel? You have received the Bible from the Catholic Church: you know that the Bible is the Bible, the inspired word of God, only because you have received it as such from the infallible authority of the Catholic Church.

From the Bible itself you cannot prove its inspiration. You cannot discover in it a list of the inspired books. You cite in vain such passages as the following from the second Epistle to Timothy: "All Scripture is divinely inspired." Neither this nor any other passage tells you whether this or that particular book is of Divine inspiration: the precise books that are to be received as the inspired word of God, you can only learn from the Catholic Church. St. Augustine was right in saying, "I would not believe in the Gospel, if the authority of the Church did not oblige me to do so."

You maintain that the Church from whom you have received the Bible, is essentially corrupt: how then do you know that she has not unscrupulously falsified or interpolated it, as Luther did in the famous passage of the Epistle to the Romans, "We account a man to be justified by faith," to which Luther added the word "alone." If the Church was in error for a thousand years, as you maintain, who can assure you that during so long a period of wilful corruption, she did not change, remodel, mutilate, or at least interpolate the Scripture? You do not accuse the Church of having falsified the Bible; your silence is an implicit admission, that she has seen nothing in it that contradicts her claims; and such is the real state of the case.

Once more I affirm that without the Catholic Church you cannot know that the Bible is an inspired book. If Luther and the early Reformers had claimed that they had received the Bible from the hands of an angel, as Mahomet claimed for the Koran, Protestantism would have some show of consistency: as it is, Protestantism contradicts itself, and must either acknowledge the infallibility of the Catholic Church, or give up the inspiration of the Bible

But admitting for the sake of argument, that you could know from other sources that the Bible is the inspired word of God, still you cannot assume it as a Rule of Faith. A Rule of Faith ought to be clear, complete from the beginning of its existence, universal, accessible to every one, and capable of settling all disputes relating to faith.

. A Rule of Faith must be *clear* to every

body, for as the faith is intended for all men, the Rule of Faith must be adapted to the comprehension of all, easily and perfectly intelligible to the meanest capacity, because faith is incompatible with religious doubt.

Is the Bible easily intelligible, clear to every one? Evidently not. To pretend that it is enough to read it to be fully instructed in every thing necessary for salvation, is as extravagant as to maintain that to be a man of learning it is enough to buy a scientific work and read it, without preparatory training or guidance.

St. Peter says, speaking of the Epistles of St. Paul, that in them there are, " some things hard to be understood, and which the unlearned and unstable wrest, as also the other Scriptures, to their own perdition."* Universal experience testifies to the obscurity of many passages of the Bible. The Jews misunderstood the Old Testament. With the Bible in their hands, they did not recognize in Christ the Messiah foretold by the prophets; they rejected and crucified Him. During the Christian era, the Bible has been misunderstood in all ages by those who have rejected the

* 2 Pet., iii. 16.

authority of the Catholic Church. St. Jerome remarked fifteen hundred years ago, "By texts of Scripture every heretic has always found means to bolster up his errors." St. Augustine, at a somewhat later period, made a similar remark: "How do so many heresies arise," he asks, "but because the Scripture, though good in itself, is not rightly understood?" You know the history of the eunuch of Candace, related in the Acts. When Philip asked him whether he understood the prophet Isaiah whom he was reading, the eunuch asked him with astonishment, "How can I, unless some one show me?"* If a man of education, who spoke a kindred language, could not understand Isaiah at that time, how can men at the present day pretend to understand the whole Scripture without guide or comment? St. Jerome was so shocked at the presumptuous assurance of the heretics of his time, that he exclaimed indignantly, "Carpenters stick to their own trade, cooks to their kitchen, but the Scriptures every one thinks himself competent to explain!" How would that learned Father of the Church have spoken, had some one in his day presumed to set up the private inter-

* Acts, viii. 31.

pretation of the Bible as the only Rule of Faith? Yet you maintain that all mankind, those who cannot read as well as those who can, must rely for their faith on their own private interpretation of the Bible. And what is still more astonishing is, that, by your own admission, Private Interpretation is fallible. If fallible, it cannot be the Rule of Faith, for faith excludes doubt, and fallibility does not.

2. A Rule of Faith must be *complete*, that is, it must contain every article of Faith. This is not the case with the Bible. St. John says at the close of his Gospel, " There are also many other things which Jesus did, which if they were written every one, the world itself, I think, would not be able to contain the books that should be written." It is evident that Christ, in his three years of public life, must have taught much that is not recorded in the Gospels. So with the Apostles. They preached the faith all over the world, as St. Paul testifies in his epistle to the Colossians,* yet but few of them wrote anything at all, and what they did write besides the Gospels, Acts, Apocalypse, was in the form of occasional Epistles; not one of them has left us a complete systematic treatise on faith. In their Epistles, they fre-

---

* Colos., i. 5, 6.

quently refer to their oral teachings, and attach just as much importance to these as to their writings. St. Paul says, "Therefore, brethren, stand firm: and hold the traditions which you have learned, whether by word or by our epistle."* St. John says, "I had many things to write unto thee, but I would not by ink and pen write to thee. But I hope speedily to see thee; and we will speak face to face."† Will you maintain that all that Christ and the Apostles ever taught or preached, beyond what has been written, was of no importance, and contained nothing pertaining to the faith?

Tell me why you baptize infants, though there is not a word about infant baptism in the whole Scripture? and why you do not wash one another's feet, although Christ apparently commands the practice as necessary for salvation? Christ said to Peter, "If I wash thee not, thou shalt have no part with me," and to all the Apostles, "You also ought to wash one another's feet." You administer infant baptism, and omit the other practice, because the Tradition of the Catholic Church has taught you, that the baptism of infants is necessary

---

* 2 Thess. ii. 14. See also, 1 Cor. xi. 2, 2 Thess. iii. 6. 2 Tim. i. 13; ii. 2; iii. 14.

† 3 John, 13, 14.

for their salvation, but the washing of one another's feet was not commanded as an indispensable rite. Relinquishing the letter of the Bible on these points, and throwing yourself back on Tradition, why do you maintain that the Bible is the only Rule of Faith? Your practice, as well as your theory, is inconsistent with itself.

3. A Rule of Faith must be as *old* as the faith itself. But the Bible, by its own testimony, is not so old. Christ sent His Apostles to preach, not to write: "He that heareth you heareth me."* Their mission was symbolized by the fiery tongues under the appearance of which the Holy Ghost descended upon them. They did not leave us in the Bible any system of faith regularly and purposely drawn up. Not a word of the New Testament was written for seven years after the first preaching of the Gospel; the last book was not in existence till the sixty-fourth year after the Ascension. There were false gospels circulated as well as true ones, and it was only in the fourth century, by the solemn definition of the first General Council, that it became authentically known what books were to be received as truly

* Luke, x. 16.

inspired. If the Bible is the Rule of Faith, then there was no faith for seven years after the Apostles had begun their mission, no faith during nearly the whole of the first century, none during the first three hundred years of the Christian era, for the Bible was not complete before the close of the first century, and not authentically known as inspired until the fourth. What cannot have been the Rule of Faith from the beginning, cannot be the Rule of Faith now, for no new Revelation has been made since the time of Christ. It was only after the period of the persecutions, when peace was given to the Church, that the canon of the genuine books of Scripture was drawn up by the Church assembled in General Council at Nice, A.D. 325. Would you say that the exemplary Christians of the Apostolic age, the first fruits of Christianity, possessed only a fragmentary, uncertain Rule of Faith, or none at all? If so, they were only imperfectly Christian, or not Christians at all. In the second century, St. Irenæus, a disciple of St. Polycarp who had himself been a disciple of St. John the Apostle, informs us, that in his time there were whole nations who had never read a word of Holy Writ, and yet were excellent Christians.

4. A Rule of Faith must be *universal*, for Christ revealed the faith for all men and for all time, and "without faith no one can be saved." Does the Bible possess the character of universality? Evidently not, for by far the greater portion of mankind cannot even read. How could any one ever attribute to the infinite wisdom of God a Rule of Faith, which, though necessary for salvation, is yet such that it is perfectly unavailable for the immense majority of men?

If the Scripture is the only Rule of Faith, and consequently necessary for salvation, it is not enough to read portions of the Bible: every one is obliged to read the whole of it, for otherwise he would be in manifest danger of overlooking many things that are essential for salvation. Do you pretend to say that every Protestant reads the whole Bible, or considers himself obliged to do so?

All men can hear the faith preached, but there never was a time when all could read. As certain as it is that Christ has revealed the faith for all mankind, and has commanded all to hear it; as certain as it is that all cannot read, and that among those who can read, there are few who can read the Bible in the original languages in which it was written; so certain it is, that the Bible is not the Rule of Faith. It is not the Rule of Faith for those who cannot read, simply because they are unable to read the Bible; nor for those who cannot read it in the original Hebrew and Greek, because they can obtain no certainty that their translation is, in all respects, a faithful rendering of the original.

You may allege that those who cannot read, may hear the Bible read by others. But every ignorant man has not the opportunity of hearing the Bible read, and, if he had, it would be unsatisfactory, for he would have to rely implicitly on the honesty of the reader; he would be completely dependent for his faith, not on an infallible authority, but on one who may imitate the example of Luther, and perhaps go so far as to interpolate the Bible to make it agree with his own private opinions. But suppose the readers as honest as you please, still the Bible cannot be the Rule of Faith for the ignorant; it is not the Rule of Faith even for the most enlightened.

5. A Rule of Faith must be *accessible* to every one, but the Bible was not generally accessible before the fifteenth century. Until the middle of the fifteenth century, when the art of printing was invented, the seventy-five

books of Scripture had to be copied with immense labor; complete copies of the Bible were so scarce, and the price of them so high, that only ecclesiastics and rich people could procure them. Has Christ come only for ecclesiastics and the rich? If the Bible is the Rule of Faith, hardly a single poor man for almost fifteen centuries could have been a Christian. Even at the present day, the Bible is not within the reach of every body. Dr. Ives, formerly an Episcopalian Bishop, now a fervent convert to the Catholic faith, has made the following striking and just remark: "Christ assures us that ' to the poor the Gospel is preached,' yet if the Bible is the Rule of Faith instituted by Christ, then the poor are in a worse condition than the rich." Your Bible Associations, intended to remedy the evil, supply the proof of the assertion; but for the press the Bible would still be a rare book.

If your doctrine is true, Christ has not sufficiently provided for men's salvation. Alphonso of Arragon once had the audacity, in his philosophical pride, to utter the blasphemy that if he had been present at the creation of the world, he would have given God many a good advice. He had scarcely ended when a fearful thunderstorm arose; vivid flashes of lightning struck nearer and nearer around the palace; the king was terrified, and retracted his blasphemy.

To maintain that the Bible is the Rule of Faith, is to hold, by implication, that God has failed to establish sufficient means of salvation; it implies that He should have had recourse to the advice of men. Your principle when carried to its legitimate consequences, obliges you to say, that God should have given the Bible to men from the beginning, placed it within the reach of every man in every age, and made it so clear as to be easily intelligible to the meanest capacity, and incapable of being misunderstood by any. He should have bestowed on men the faculty of reading as well as that of hearing, and given them the press together with the Bible.

But this, I presume, in your view as well as in ours, is blasphemy; you disclaim it, and yet, if your principle is true, it is an inference which, it would appear, must be obvious to every reflecting mind. The principle itself, therefore, is untenable. God has no need of our advice. He has given us the Scripture as one of the channels of our faith, and as such it is a precious gift; but not as a Rule of Faith, for it is evidently unfit for that purpose. The doctrine that the Bible is the Rule of Faith, contradicts the wisdom of God, as will become clearer still from the sixth characteristic which a Rule of Faith must possess.

6. A Rule of Faith must be capable of *settling* every dispute that may arise upon any article of faith. The Bible cannot do this. It is not a book which is its own interpreter.

What would you think of the plan of abolishing all courts of law, and substituting for them a law book, with the declaration that every one should read it to ascertain his rights, and that all disputes must be settled by the private interpretation of the text? With such a plan no quarrel would ever end. And what, if the book, though written for the use of all, yet demanded great learning to be properly understood? What, if instead of being written in plain English, it was written in Hebrew and Greek? The idea is ridiculous. It would be just as unwise on the part of God to have made the Bible the Rule of Faith for all nations, times, and tongues, as for a lawgiver to abolish all courts of justice, and substitute for them a code of laws written in a foreign language. You shrink with horror from the idea of attributing a want of wisdom to God, yet such is the logical inference from your doctrine that the Bible, without any living judge to interpret it, is the Rule of Faith.

What Goethe has said to ridicule quibbling trancendentalists, is applicable here. "Those speculators," he says, "are like animals led about by a wicked spirit in a sandy circle, while all around them there is a green meadow." Your Private Interpretation of the Bible leads you round in the arid wastes of fruitless speculation, while near you, full in view, God has placed the infallible authority of the Church that would lead you to the fields of life-giving truth contained in His written and unwritten Word.

The Bible has not a single one of the characteristics of a Rule of Faith: your fundamental principle must be rejected. As a channel of Divine Revelation, the Bible is a most precious gift of God; as such it has always been recognized and used by the Catholic Church; she has had no reason to reject or alter it. As such it bears witness to the validity of her claims: she has a right to address you in the words of Scripture, "Search the Scriptures: for you think in them to have life everlasting: and the same are they that render testimony of me." If you really believe that the Bible is the Word of God, search the

Bible with candor, and you will become satisfied that the Catholic Church is the only true Church of Christ; that she is the infallible interpreter of the Word of God, and that to her decisions you are bound in conscience to submit. "If he will not hear the Church, let him be to thee as the heathen and the publican."* What Church does Christ mean? Evidently the Church which He built on Peter, "Thou art Peter, and upon this rock I will build my Church; and the gates of hell shall not prevail against it."† That Church, as I have fully proved to you, is the Catholic Church alone. The Bible condemns your separation from her, denies that it is the Rule of Faith, and makes it a matter, not of choice, but of necessity, to hear the Church. Why then, do you remain out of the communion of the Catholic Church? What hinders you from perceiving the wrongs which you have suffered at the hands of the Reformers? What prevents you from returning to the Church from which you were separated by the blind fury of passion and despotism?

The first reason that keeps you out of the Catholic Church, is a lack of earnest examina

* Matt., xviii. 17.
† Matt., xvi. 18.

tion, especially in regard to the principle of faith: I have therefore given you the refutation of the Protestant principle of faith, and the proofs of the Divine character of the Catholic Church and of her Infallibility in matters of faith. Have you earnestly examined my proofs? Another reason is prejudice: I will proceed to show you, as briefly and clearly as possible, that all your objections are unfounded, and that instead of truth you believe calumnies.

CHAPTER III.

PROTESTANT PREJUDICES.

If all that you have ever heard and read against the Catholic Church, against her faith, her Popes, Bishops, and Priests, were true, you would have a good reason for your separation. But you believe calumnies; and where is the fault to be sought for? Not in the Catholic Church, but in your adopting without examination almost any charge brought against us. From your earliest infancy you have heard fabulous accounts of Catholic faith and practice; you learned to lisp them on your mothers' lap; your hair has grown gray, you have reached the brink of the grave, in the firm belief of imputations as groundless as they are enormous. Millions of Protestants carry their anti-Catholic prejudices to the tomb. The power of preconceived opinions is so great, that it often prevents men of the highest intelligence and education from perceiving the most obvious truths. Did you ever reflect on the astonishing effect of prejudices? They may be trifling in themselves, but their power to impede the perception of truth is enormous. Numberless illustrations of this fact occur in familiar objects.

A piece of worthless cloth placed before the window darkens the room at midday; a cloud obscures the light of the sun; a beam thrown across the railtrack hurls the train down the embankment; a little dust blinds the eye of the eagle. It is so with prejudice. If a man is under the influence of prejudice, you may reason with him as much as you please, you labor in vain. For him the clearest light is darkness; logic only serves to drive him more deeply into error.

Of the effect of prejudice, where it exists, there can be no doubt; but with regard to the origin and continuance of the prejudices against the Catholic Church, I do not know which is more surprising, the effrontery of those who invented and spread the calumnies, or the narrowness of mind which has believed and transmitted them for centuries without inquiry. Did I not know it from personal experience, I could hardly have credited that such ideas as actually exist about Catholics and their Church, could ever have been accepted or invented.

I have met with a respectable, well-educated Protestant lady who confessed to me, that for many years she had entertained the idea that Catholics had goats' feet. The first time she saw a Catholic, she instinctively looked at his feet, to see whether they were human or not.

On the other hand, while it is undeniable that there are Protestant writers and speakers guilty of maliciously spreading the most absurd and atrocious calumnies against us; the candor, the perfect fairness and honesty with which Catholics universally treat Protestant doctrines, cannot fail to exert on your minds a powerful influence in favor of the Catholic faith. You cannot cite a single instance of a Catholic writer misrepresenting your opinions; there never was an instance of it. Yet there is hardly a Catholic doctrine which has not been distorted, presented under an aspect which we abhor as much as you do, or replaced by some monstrous tenet never dreamed of in the Catholic Church. In reviewing the popular prejudices against the Catholic Church, I shall have occasion to give you many striking proofs of this fact; but before proceeding further, I must quote an extract from an able article in a Catholic paper, *The Toronto Freeman:*

"Whilst Protestants reject the unwritten word of God, as of no authority,—whilst they boast that they build their faith on the written Word alone, and condemn only what it condemns—they yet are the victims of a hateful tradition, that is at variance with the first principles of Christianity. This great Protestant *tradition* consists in misrepresenting Catholic doctrines, and in imputing to the Church acts and teachings that she abhors. With the great mass of non-Catholics, this tradition is of equal authority with the Bible, and is far more efficacious in chaining them to their errors and delusions. It is necessary for the very existence of Protestantism. 'Truth,' says Milton, 'is powerful next to the Almighty,' and error is impotent in its presence. Truth has a charm for the mind of man,—it is its life, its food, and it attracts the soul towards it as the north the mariner's needle. Error, therefore, to subsist at all, must not cope with truth, as such,—it must, by the very instinct of self-preservation, be dim, and hide the bright radiance of truth beneath the dark cloak of calumny—it must misrepresent—it must distort and disfigure it—it must cover its fair face with a hideous mask, and thus frighten men from its contemplation. Protestantism has been true to this instinct of self-preservation. Since the day it burst forth, like an impure stream, from the corrupt hearts of the so-called Reformers, it has lived on calumny and misrepresentation. Truth could not answer its purposes—because truth would be its condemnation; it has, therefore, had recourse to slander, in all its contests with the Church. 'The Pope,' it cries, ' is anti-Christ. Papists adore images, and give divine honor to Saints and Angels. They are benighted and priest-ridden. The Priests give license to commit sin ; nay, they even give permission to murder the enemies of the Church. The Church of Rome is the enemy of the Word of God—she chains the intellect and enslaves the soul.' These are but the beginning of the long litany of lying accusations made by Protestantism against the Church. They constitute the burden of many a long-winded oration, in pulpits and on platforms ; and many a time the white of an eye is turned heavenward at

the recital of the abominations of Popery. But
this huge swindle on men's minds is beginning
to be exploded. Men at length dare to disbelieve the great Protestant tradition. Noble
minds are rising above the level of vulgar prejudice, and are daily won to the Church, after
a strict investigation into her title-deeds. Two
works have been written by recent converts—
men of mind and of position in society—and
men, besides, who could have no worldly interest as the motive of their conversion. The
author of 'The Path which led a Protestant
Lawyer to the Church,'—Peter H. Burnett—
examined into the real doctrines of the Church,
and was startled at finding himself to have
been so long the victim of wicked misrepresentation. Hear what the learned author says
on the matter: 'This system,' he says, page
700, ' of misrepresentation of Catholic doctrines,
practices, and intentions, so general among
Protestant writers, gave rise, in my mind, to
very serious questions. Why did SUCCESS originally require such a line of argument? Why
did *truth* require such a support? Why was
such a course preferred, in support of an
alleged true system? And why is it still
necessary? Are bad arguments more effective
than good? Is misrepresentation better, in a

good cause, than candor and truth? If the doctrines really held by Catholics were so false, erroneous, and absurd, did they need exaggeration, to cause their rejection? Does the grossest error, or error of any kind, require to be darkened beyond its real demerits, to make it hated and despised? And is it necessary to prepare the human mind for the reception of truth, that it should first be filled with falsehood? Do you sow *weeds* before you sow good grain? Is it necessary in order to inculcate charity, that you should first give a proof of its absence in the party who inculcates it? And if you wish to put down falsehood, is it necessary, by your own act, to show its *utility and necessity?* True, it is a practical rule with too many, to use falsehood against alleged falsehood, according to the common maxim, that you must oppose the devil with fire. But is this Christianity? is it true philosophy? On the contrary, is it not the doctrine of revenge? the practice of savages? the chief maxim of morality among wolves and tigers? And if you wish to vanquish the evil spirit and his bad cause, had you not better fight him with something the opposite of that which he uses himself? Had you not better oppose evil with good? But does not the NECESSITY arise from other causes? Is it because there is a unity—a force—a beauty in the Catholic system, that renders it logically impregnable? Is it because it is conformable to the truth of Christianity, JUST AS IT IS, and not as the passions, interests, and pride of men would make it, that the Catholic theory is so much misrepresented and despised? Why is it that every proud innovator upon a permanent system—every wild fanatic—every demagogue in religion—every sect, and the broken fragments of every sect, from Simon Magus to the present time, have one and all been down upon the Church?"

"In the preface to his elaborate and well-reasoned essay, 'On the Harmonious Relations between Divine Faith and Natural Religion,' Judge Baine—a distinguished convert of Stockton, California—thus discourses of the injustice of that system of misrepresentation of which we have been speaking:—"It is a principle of universal jurisprudence, that no man, not even the most lowly culprit, shall be condemned unheard, no matter how fierce his accusers may be, and no matter how terrible the crimes they may lay to his charge. The judge who would condemn a man upon mere clamor, without any investigation into the actual conduct of the person accused, would be considered both cruel and unjust. And the Church feels most profoundly and earnestly insists that whoever denounces her teaching, without learning from her own standard of faith exactly what she does teach as Divine faith, is at once unjust to her and to his own intellect and soul.' Alluding to that oft-repeated calumny, that the Church cramps the intellect and enslaves the body, he says :—'It has been the accusation of ages against the Church, that she usurps the provinces of reason, common sense, and experience, in teaching Divine faith to her children; and millions upon millions of men have accepted the accusation as true, without ever having seen one of her catechisms, or any standard of her faith, written by one of her recognized teachers. Indeed, her accusers doom her to their hate even without consulting her theologians and historians—so that they are ignorant of both her faith and her theology. And I respectfully appeal to any one who now condemns her, whether they do so because they have read and understood the teaching of her authorized doctors; or whether they do it upon the historical assertions of her enemies, and their denunciations of her faith.'"

I shall now rapidly glance at the most common American prejudices against the Catholic

Church. They may be divided into religious and political prejudices, or prejudices of Americans as Protestants, and their prejudices as Citizens. In refuting your prejudices, I shall occasionally refer to remarks which I made in the first chapter, when I considered the consolations of Catholic doctrines as compared with the distressing nature of Protestant tenets; I shall be obliged to reiterate some of those observations, in order to correct the erroneous views which many of you entertain respecting Catholic belief and practice.

SECTION I.

RELIGIOUS PREJUDICES.

THE POPE.

You have been taught that Catholics are obliged by their faith to believe as infallible truth whatever the Pope says, and to execute whatever he commands. This idea is false; it is an utterly unfounded prejudice. The genuine Catholic doctrine is, that the Church, with the Pope, is infallible in matters of faith only, and only when she solemnly defines an article of faith. When the Pope writes or speaks as a private doctor, he is liable to error; but when in his official capacity, as Head of the whole Church, he defines an article of faith, we hold him to be infallible. This doctrine is based on the solemn promise of Christ to Peter, "I have prayed for thee, that thy faith fail not: and thou being once converted confirm thy brethren,"* and other similar promises of Christ, made to Peter as Head of the Church, and through him to his successors: the texts have been repeatedly cited in the preceding pages. As we have seen, the very idea of the Church founded by Christ to be the religious guide and instructor of man to the end of time, involves the necessity of an infallible authority in the Head of the Church to settle controverted points of doctrine.

To illustrate our doctrine, I may repeat a remark of Count de Maistre, in his work entitled *Du Pape*:—" Civil society," he says, " is forced to set up a tribunal infallible *de facto*, for the preservation of social order." In America you have the Supreme Court of the United States, established as a final tribunal, from whose decision there lies no appeal. Its decisions, therefore, are adopted as infallible *de facto*. Such an institution is absolutely necessary, for otherwise there never would be an end to litigation. Its infallibility is only a legal and political fiction, indispensable to the

* Luke, xxii. 32.

preservation of the public peace or the union of States. In the Church, the infallibility of the supreme tribunal, in matters of faith, is not a fiction, but from the very nature of the case must be an infallible truth, for the true Church of Christ, as I have shown, cannot change, and error in the faith would be an essential change.

The Church of Christ is the Kingdom of Truth. When Pilate asked Jesus, " Art thou a King, then ? Jesus answered: Thou sayest that I am a King. For this was I born, and for this came I into the world ; that I should give testimony to the truth : every one that is of the truth heareth my voice."*

I do not understand how you can make any objection to the doctrine of Papal Infallibility, while, in the political and civil order, you are forced, and all nations are forced, to adopt an infallibility *de facto* in the Supreme Court. The infallibility of the Church has reference to objects of infinitely higher moment : it gives us security in our eternal interests.

Though the official infallibility of the Pope, s clearly deducible from the Scripture, and follows from the decisions of General Councils, and is moreover irresistibly proved by logical

---

* John, xviii. 37.

inference, yet it must be observed that it has never been defined as an article of Catholic Faith, and consequently no one becomes a heretic, in this respect, unless he denies the nfallibility of the whole Church in union with the Pope.

THE CLERGY.

You have been taught that Catholic Priests perform their sacred functions for money, make a traffic of Confession and Absolution, and sell the permission to commit sin. All this is a calumny. It is true that on occasion of marriages, baptisms, funerals, and when a Mass is asked to be offered for a particular intention, it is usual for Catholics to give a gratuity to their Pastors; the sum is commonly very small, and it is neither offered nor accepted as an exchange for spirituals, but as a contribution for the support of the Pastor.

It was enjoined in the Old Law, and St. Paul repeats the injunction, " that they who work in the holy place, eat the things that are of the holy place: and they who serve at the altar, partake of the altar. So also the Lord ordained that they who preach the gospel, should live of the gospel."* It is but just that the people should contribute for the support of the Priest, who, if he had not chosen the ministry, would, in most cases, have been better able to provide for himself in some other profession. The Jews were obliged to give the tenth part of their income to the Temple: if Catholics, of their own accord, paid tithes in this sense, they would only do what the Old Law enjoined on the Jews; but there is not a single Catholic congregation which contributes to that extent, or from which so much is demanded or expected. Priests, especially in this country, are scantily and often miserably provided for; their privations here are so great, in most cases, that this may be assigned as one of the reasons why there are comparatively few native Americans among the Catholic Priesthood.

When you accuse Catholic Priests of a money-making spirit, might not the reproach be turned against Protestant ministers? I am unwilling to recriminate, but 1 must ask you Which are better provided for, Catholic priests or Protestant ministers? I need not give the

---
* 1 Cor., ix. 13, 14.

answer. If you look back to your mother country, England, you will see a still more striking contrast. The immense wealth of the High Church is universally known. That wealth, while it was in the hands of the Catholic clergy, served to provide for the wants of the needy: is it so at the present day? Read Cobbett's "History of the Reformation," and you will never again reproach the Catholic clergy with a money-seeking spirit.

The Church obliges no one to pay for the administration of the Sacraments. As is done among you, Catholics on occasion of Baptism contribute for the support of the Pastor, but they are not obliged to do so on that occasion; they may do it at any other time at their convenience. But no money is ever received for Confessions: all you hear on that subject against us is a calumny. Unfortunately the calumny is very common.

In 1859, I was traveling through the State of Mississippi in the cars. The railroad to New Orleans was not yet completed: so one evening we were forced to wait, in the middle of the woods, for stage-coaches to convey us to the next terminus. I hired a man to accompany me to the nearest hotel. While passing over a log thrown across a deep trench, the man looked back at me and asked, "Who are you, sir?" "I am a Catholic Priest." "A Catholic Priest!" he exclaimed in a tone of voice that denoted intense hatred, and with an air of contempt and abhorrence, "I hate Catholic Priests." My situation in that lonely place, in the presence of a stout man and bitter enemy, was by no means pleasant. I replied calmly, "If all that you have heard about Catholic Priests were true, I should hate them more than you do. But believe me, it is all prejudice and calumny." "Why," said he, in a rage, "don't you Priests forgive sins for money?" "Friend, look at me, and see whether I am sincere. I was a Priest before you were born, and have heard many a hundred thousand Confessions; and I now declare before God, that I have never in my whole life received a cent for all the Confessions I have heard in Europe or America." My answer satisfied him; he became calm and polite, and asked me many questions about the Catholic religion. On arriving at the hotel, I paid him liberally for his services. After supper I had a remarkable proof of his extraordinary change of sentiments towards Catholic Priests. Entering the parlor, where a large number of gentlemen were assembled he asked them in a solemn tone of voice, "Gentlemen, do you believe there is a true Christian on earth?" The company burst out into a laugh; some asked him, "Do you think yourself that one true Christian?" Pointing me out, he said, "I think, if there is a true Christian on earth, it is that Priest." So quickly had his hatred been changed into an exaggerated affection.

If Americans in general would take the trouble of conversing with Catholic Priests, or reading our books, their anti-Catholic prejudices would at once vanish, and their aversion change into affection.

CONFESSION.

You have been taught that Confession is an invention of the Priesthood, and that the primitive Christians never heard of such an institution. This is an error. Confession and the duty of confessing are as old as the words of Christ, "Receive ye the Holy Ghost: whose sins you shall forgive, they are forgiven them, and whose you shall retain, they are retained."[*]

[*] John, xx. 22, 23.

How could the Apostles have discharged the duty of forgiving or retaining sins, if the early Christians were not obliged to confess their sins? The Apostles were not omniscient, and their authority of forgiving or retaining sins could not be exercised, unless the faithful declared their hidden offences.

If Christ had merely said, "Whose sins you shall forgive, they are forgiven," the case would have been different: the Apostles and priests of the Church could then have forgiven sin without confession; but Christ added, "Whose sins you shall retain, they are retained." The power conferred is a discretionary power; neither Priest nor Apostle could ever have exercised it prudently or justly, except upon an accurate knowledge of the conscience of the penitent: absolution or denial of absolution must necessarily, from the nature of the case, depend upon the avowal of the penitent, for he alone can make the state of his conscience accurately known. To apply these words of our Lord to the preaching of the Gospel in order to move men to Contrition, is utterly ridiculous, for, what would then be the meaning of the words, "whose sins you shall retain, they are retained?"

If you insist that Confession is an invention

of the Priests, you must be able to assign the date when it was first introduced, and the name of the inventor. This you can never do. The most ancient among the Fathers of the Church speak of Confession as an institution that had existed from the beginning of Christianity. Tertullian, who lived in the second century of our era, speaks of Confession as clearly as we do at the present day. In his work "*De Pænitentia*" he says, "I think there are some who shun this [Confession], as an exposure of themselves, or put it off from day to day, thinking more of the shame than of their cure; like those who, affected with some disease, conceal it from the physician, and perish through shame."[*] St. Irenæus, St. Cyprian, Origen, and many more of the most ancient Fathers, speak of Confession in the same explicit manner. St. Clement of Rome, a cotemporary of St. John the Apostle, urges the faithful to confess their sins to the Priests, in order to be reconciled to God through their means.

If Confession were an invention of the Priests, they would not have imposed the obligation of Confession upon themselves, but only on the laity; the law, however, is general, binding as

[*] De Pænit., ix. x.

well on Priests, Bishops, and the Pope, as on laymen. All are equally obliged to confess their sins.

If Confession has not come down from the Apostles, the innovation, like all heresies, must have left a distinct mark in history; a universal outcry must have been raised against the bold innovator who first attempted to oblige the whole of Christendom, including the Pope himself, to confess their most secret offences to a man like themselves.

In 1856, on board a steamboat on Lake Michigan, a Methodist preacher asked me, " Are you a Catholic Priest ?" " Yes, sir, I am ?" " May I ask you a question ?" " Certainly." " Does the Pope go to Confession ?" " Of course he does, for if he were not obliged to do it, no one would be. The Pope as a man is liable to fall. Christ did not institute a Church for him different from the one of which he is the head." " To whom does he confess? Does he confess to the Lord Jesus Christ?" continued the astonished preacher. " No, sir, he confesses to a Priest, and he might confess to me." " I never heard that before," exclaimed the preacher, with increasing wonder. " I wish, sir, you would ask me some more questions about the Catholic Church, for there are many other things, I am sure, which you have never heard." This first discovery, however, was too much for him; he had not the courage to proceed.

There are but too many Protestants who act in the same way; the want of earnest investigation is the great evil. Many ask, like Pilate, " What is the truth?" but turn their back without waiting for an answer, and live and die in their erroneous religious opinions and prejudices. Some, I doubt not, who will take up this short work of mine, will throw it aside after having read a few pages: if such men remain in error it is their own fault; they are evidently unwilling to know the truth.

You have always thought that Confession is an intolerable burden. I have shown you in another portion of this book, that Confession is, in reality, a source of consolation, peace, light, and strength; I need not repeat the remarks I have already made, and, indeed, if you wish to be convinced of the truth of my assertion, you need only ask any devout Catholic, and you will find that I have but stated the universal experience of all who have ever made a good confession.

INDULGENCES.

You have been taught, and many among you believe, that an Indulgence means a license to-commit sin, and is granted for money by the Priests to any Catholic who applies for it. This is a malicious calumny. As every Catholic child and every Catholic Catechism could inform you, and as I remarked in speaking of this subject before, an Indulgence has nothing at all to do with the remission of sins; an Indulgence is nothing more than a remission of temporal punishments remaining due to sin after absolution. It presupposes contrition, penance, the pardon of sin, and a heart free from all deliberate attachment to sin. Indeed, an Indulgence with permission to commit sin is a most glaring contradiction, although you take the two expressions to be synonymous, and imagine the Catholic Church teaches your opinion.

I might retort with truth that the original Protestant doctrine of saving faith, the doctrine that we are saved by faith alone, in spite of sin, and without repentance, is, indeed, a permission to commit sin, of which Luther's scandalous advice is only a legitimate deduction,—" Sin, but believe all the more firmly."

THE BIBLE.

You have been taught that the Catholic Church is hostile to the Bible. It is a calumny. I have already reminded you of the great solicitude of the Catholic Church for preserving the Bible, before the invention of the art of printing. But for the Catholic monks, whose labors transmitted manuscript copies of it from age to age, what would have become of the New Testament?? I have also shown you, that but for the infallible testimony of the Catholic Church you would not know that the Bible is the Bible; that she can have no reason to be unfavorable to the Bible, since her own authority is proved by it, even without considering it as inspired, and only regarding it as authentic history.

The Church, you insist, does not allow the free use of the Bible; but this, also, as urged by Protestants, is a calumny. Here is the true statement of the case. The Catholic Church places some restraint on the *indiscriminate* reading of the Bible in the modern tongues, and does not generally allow it, unless the translation is accompanied by authorized notes explanatory of obscure or difficult passages. In so doing she acts with wisdom, for it is clear from all past experience that misinterpretation of the Bible may lead to the most terrific consequences, subverting faith, morality, and public order. But to say that the Catholic Church puts any obstacle to the reading of the Bible with authorized explanatory notes, and by those who can derive profit from it, is a most injurious calumny. You have an obvious refutation of it in the well-known fact, that long before Luther was born, the Bible was translated into German, French, Italian, Spanish, Bohemian, and other languages. The German translation of Augsburg had gone through eight editions, and the Italian by Malermi, through twenty-three. These translations were made for the people, and bought and read by the people.

The Catholic Church has never prevented the reading, but only the unprofitable and unguarded reading of the Bible, and in doing so, she is true to her high mission as the true Church of Christ, the guardian of faith and morality, the religious guide of men appointed by Divine Wisdom. Her precautionary measures are a proof of her reverence for the Word of God, while Protestantism, urging the reading of the Bible, without note or comment, without regard to capacity or prudence, shows rather a want of respect for the sacred volume. The conduct of the Church is not new. Fourteen or fifteen centuries ago, in the age when the canon of Scripture was first framed, St. Jerome inveighed in very energetic language against the pretension that every one is a fit interpreter of the Bible.* "Mind your sauce," said St. Basil to the imperial cook, "the Bible is above the dresser."

SAINTS.

You have been taught from your earliest childhood, that Catholics adore Saints and images. It is a calumny, destitute of all foundation in truth. Ask the first Catholic child you meet, and you will learn that Catholics adore God alone. Here is a brief outline of the Catholic doctrine.

We honor the Saints just as we honor living men of distinguished virtue; we revere them for their virtues. The honor we render them

---

* See a passage cited above.

is no doubt greater than any we give to living men, but it is of the same kind, and only greater in degree, because the Saints have persevered in virtue, and are in the enjoyment of their reward. St. Augustine, in the early ages of the Church, explained the doctrine just as we do now; among other passages, the following occurs in the twentieth book of his work against Faustus the Manichean: "We honor the martyrs with that honor of charity and fellowship, with which even in this life we honor the holy servants of God whose hearts we find ready to undergo the same sufferings for evangelic truth. But we honor them with greater devotion, because they are safer, having conquered in the strife. . . . But with that worship, which is *called adoration*, we neither honor, nor teach any man to honor any one but God alone."* Is this doctrine, in any respect, exceptionable?

We ask the Saints to intercede for us with God; but do you not ask one another's prayers on earth? Did not the Apostles ask the faithful to pray for them? Why, then, should we not have recourse to the Saints in Heaven, who are so much nearer to God? Your objections

---

* St. Aug. contra Faust. Manich. l. xx. n. xxi.

were answered many centuries ago, by St Jerome, in his short treatise against Vigilantius: "If the Apostles and Martyrs could pray for others, while they were still living in the flesh, while they were still obliged to be solicitous for themselves; how much more can they do so, after having gained the crown, the victory, the triumph! . . . Have they less power, as soon as they begin to be with Christ?"

You have been taught that the intercession of the Saints would be an injury offered to Christ. It is the very reverse. We honor the Saints for the sake of Christ, through whose grace they became holy, we ask their prayers in view of the merits of Christ, through whom they intercede for us, and whose merits alone can make their intercession efficacious. "We honor the servants," says St. Augustine, in a letter to Riparius, "in order that the honor may return to the Lord."

This holy bond of mutual love, by which Christ has united the members of His Church is a powerful means of sanctification for men for the veneration and intercession of Saints constantly serve to recall to their minds examples of heroic holiness and urge them on to the practice of virtue.

Look at a well-educated family; do you not consider it a beautiful evidence of mutual affection in children, when each is ready to ask a favor for the other? Do you not prefer such a family to those in which one child roughly says to the other, Go, and ask for yourself? Parents, you who can feel the warmth and tenderness, the beautiful love of children, I leave it to you to make the application. The Church teaches nothing more in regard to the intercession of Saints, than you daily witness in your families. We are the family of God; Christ is our Head, the first-born of God, our eldest brother, through whom alone each and all of us, saints and sinners, can gain access to the mercy of God. Every one, if he chooses, may address his prayers directly to Christ, and through Christ to the Father: the Church only teaches that the intercession of Saints, if rightly understood and practiced properly, is lawful, praiseworthy, and beneficial.

We honor the images of Saints. You have been taught that we adore them. It is a malignant slander. We honor the images of Saints, as you honor the statues and pictures of your parents or of the great benefactors of the nation or of mankind. The nature of our veneration for the images of Saints was solemnly declared by the whole Church in the seventh General Council. held at Nice in the year 787. "The respect which we show to images," says that Council, "passes to the object of which they are representations." We do not adore Saints, neither do we adore their images.

You have been told that our practice is contrary to the first commandment, "Thou shalt not make to thyself a graven thing, nor the likeness of anything. . . . Thou shalt not adore them, nor serve them." I am astonished that this text should ever have been quoted against us; it is a clear proof of insincerity, and hatred of the truth, at least in those who first brought it forward in proof against the veneration of images. The text limits its own meaning: "Thou shalt not *adore* them, nor *serve* them." Do Catholics adore, do they serve images? They do not. To honor images as we do, to keep them in our houses and churches, is not to adore them. You cannot condemn us, unless you are willing to condemn God, for God ordered two cherubs to be placed in the Temple upon the ark. If the text is to be understood without limitation, then it condemns as idolatrous the making of all pictures and statues; then painters and sculptors are idolaters; then all are idolaters who have a statue or a painting of a parent, friend, or illustrious man in their houses. Nothing more is needed to show that many Protestants are not sincere in their accusations, than the charge of idolatry which they bring against us: this puts the malignity of their calumnies in a glaring light. The accusation is not new; it was made in early times by Vigilantius, who condemned the veneration of images as you do. St. Jerome met the calumny with indignation * What would St. Jerome and the early Fathers say, were they to return amongst us now, when, in spite of all the works published in explanation of the Catholic doctrine, the old accusation is constantly renewed, as if it had never been refuted? The school-house, the pulpit, and the press conspire to perpetuate the atrocious slander.

I ask you, honest and candid Americans, is it Christian or manly to inculcate such falsehoods into the minds of unsuspecting youth, to repeat them continually before ignorant multitudes, to utter them in the presence of God in your religious assemblies, and that, too, with the full consciousness of calumny?? If you

---

* See St. Jerome's Letter and Treatise against Vigilantius.

think we are in error, meet us fairly; refute what we really teach; do not object against us what we condemn and abhor as much as you do.

MARY.

Protestant misrepresentation is particularly directed against our veneration of the Blessed Virgin Mary the Mother of God. You have been taught that we adore her. It is an unfounded calumny, like the rest. Our doctrine to-day is what it was in the beginning of Christianity, and has been in all ages since; we teach to-day what St. Epiphanius taught in opposition to the heretics of the fourth century, "We honor Mary; but the Father, Son, and Holy Ghost alone, we adore."*

You will urge, perhaps, that we have greater confidence in Mary than in Jesus Christ. This, also, is a calumny. We hold that whatever power the intercession of Mary possesses with God, is derived solely from the merits of Jesus Christ: her prayers, like those of other Saints, have all their efficacy from Him and through Him.

* Epiph. Hæres. 79.

You have been told that by the doctrine of the Immaculate Conception we mean that Mary, like Jesus, was conceived of the Holy Ghost. This is simply absurd; and manifests an evident lack of good faith or information. Although Pius IX. proclaimed the Catholic doctrine solemnly and in open day, in the presence of two hundred Catholic Bishops assembled from every quarter of the globe; though the very words of the Pope were published in every Catholic journal in the country, yet the doctrine was instantly misrepresented. The Pope defined that it was a revealed truth that Mary had been conceived without incurring original sin, that is to say, that she was not at any moment defiled by the sin of our first parents. But the Protestant press and Protestant ministers throughout the whole world, represented the Pope as having defined that Mary was not conceived of man, but by the Holy Ghost. I need not give you a clearer proof of the reckless disposition to calumniate us, prevalent among the leaders of Protestantism.

We hold that Mary was exempt from original sin, because it was not becoming that the Son of God should be born of one who had ever been subject to the curse of sin and under the power of the arch-enemy of God. The doctrine is obviously in perfect accordance with reason.

Many Protestants take delight in trying to lessen the dignity of the Mother of God; their practice is a consequence of Protestant doctrine, and furnishes another proof of its inconsistency They adore the Son, and despise the Mother: can human conduct be more inconsistent? Christ has said of those who despise Him, "He that despiseth me, despiseth Him who sent me;" so we may justly say of such as despise Mary, He who does not honor the Mother, does not honor the Son. Remember the prophecy of Simeon, "Thy soul a sword shall pierce, that out of many hearts thoughts may be revealed." The disregard and contempt of Protestantism for Mary, its efforts to impair her glory, and bring her down to a level with ordinary women, all this reveals its secret tendencies, and discloses its unchristian character. There are candid men among Protestants, who acknowledge this.

In Minnesota, on the borders of the Sioux territory, I met with a French cavalry officer, who, at the time when I passed through Paris on my way to America, was engaged in the revolutionary street fights in that city. A Protestant by birth, he had married a Catholic lady, by whom he had three children, all of whom were brought up in the Catholic faith. He was himself a Catholic at heart. In the course of our conversation, he made the following remark: "What pleases me most in Catholics is that they honor Mary with so much devotion and tenderness. I was born a Protestant, but I like to hear my wife and children pray, 'Holy Mary, Mother of God, pray for us, now and at the hour of our death.' Hear what happened to me at Paris. It was during the Workmen's Revolution in 1848. General Bugeau rode up to my house, and exclaimed, 'To the barricades.' I hastily made my will, embraced my wife and children, and rode out against the rebels. The struggle was fearful. I had gone through many battles in Algiers, but the worst of them were not to be compared with this. In the midst of the hail of bullets, I thought of the prayer of my children, and on horseback, in the midst of the tumult, I prayed in my heart, Holy Mary, Mother of God, pray for me. In the hottest of the fire, I did not receive the slightest wound."

Luther rejected the veneration of Mary. He seemed to be ashamed of the salutation of the Angel, "Hail, full of grace, the Lord is with thee: Blessed are thou among women;"* and of the inspired words of Elizabeth, "Blessed art thou among women; and blessed is the fruit of thy womb;"† and of Mary's inspired prophecy, "Behold, from henceforth all generations shall call me blessed."‡ Luther has forbidden you to call Mary blessed; he has torn you from her to whose care Jesus on Calvary committed all his brethren in the person of St. John. Return to your Mother, she is the Mother of God; her compassionate hand will lead you back to Jesus, and through Him to the Father.

CELIBACY.

You object against the celibacy of the Priesthood, against the use of the Latin language in the Divine service, against our religious ceremonies. I will briefly show you that all your objections on these points are unfounded.

In regard to celibacy, I must preface what I have to say on this subject with the remark,

---

* Luke, i. 28.
† Ibid. 42.
‡ Ibid. 48.

that celibacy is not considered as a practice which is absolutely indispensable, as a law from which there can be no departure without endangering the existence of the Church. The Catholic Priests of the Greek rite are, generally speaking, married; they are not on that account excluded from the Catholic Church. But the married Greek clergy affords a strong proof of the immense advantages of celibacy; it shows clearly that celibacy enables the clergy to discharge their sacred duties with the greatest efficiency for the salvation of souls.

If you wish to know the condition of the married United Greek, or Greek Catholic, clergy, go to Gallicia on the borders of Russia. Having been there, I can bear witness that marriage has deeply impaired the dignity and influence of the clergy in that country. The people but too often experience that their married pastors are not the universal spiritual fathers of their congregations, but that "they are divided," as the Apostle says of married people, between the care of serving God, and the solicitude of pleasing their wives. It is found that a married pastor is not only divided, but is often much more anxious for the temporal interests of his family, than the spiritual welfare of his congregation; he takes more pains for the former than for the latter; domestic hindrances interfere with his pastoral duties; his wife's influence is too great, and she meddles with his spiritual functions. He is often distrusted, particularly in connection with the Sacrament of Penance: Greek Catholics, when they have the opportunity, almost always prefer to confess to an unmarried Latin priest. From your own knowledge of men, and consulting your inclinations, would you not much rather, if you had to choose, confess to an unmarried Catholic Priest than to one of your married Protestant ministers? The experiment has been tried. More than once, as you may know, certain Protestant denominations have tried to re-introduce Confession, but the people have always answered, that if Confession is necessary, they would sooner become Catholics than go to Confession to their married ministers.

The evil is still greater when a pastor has charge of several congregations, or in the case of a married Bishop who is obliged to visit his Diocese. He cannot always be at home, and jealousies and quarrels are sure to arise in consequence. The position of a married Priest becomes still more critical, if his wife leads a scandalous life, or if he has ill-bred or vicious children. When no evil of this kind exists, sickness or death in his family may at any time divert his care and attention from the wants of his congregation.

An unmarried clergy is free from all these causes of scandal, vexation, and interference with pastoral duties, and never reduced to the necessity of choosing between the interests of a family, and the religious care of a congregation.

Military discipline furnishes an apt illustration. It is not usual, in time of war, to allow soldiers to marry, and a married officer or private is considered only half a soldier. The Priesthood is a militia, the army of the Church for the defense and protection of faith and morals; and because spiritual interests are of all interests the most important, there are far more urgent reasons for an unmarried Priesthood than for an unmarried soldiery. Even Protestant denominations have occasionally expressed a wish to introduce celibacy among their clergy.*

---

* Confess. Helvet 2. c. 29. 6 Edward, c. 21.

HOLY MASS.

You object to the Mass considered as a Sacrifice, and pretend that it is an injury to the great Sacrifice of the Cross. Your objection results from a misapprehension of our doctrine. Remember what was said when I spoke of the consolation derived from the holy Sacrifice of the Mass. We do not teach that the Mass is a Sacrifice different from that of Calvary, but that it is the same Sacrifice, which Christ offers up forever for the salvation of men, the only difference being that since the Crucifixion it has been offered in an unbloody manner. We offer it because Christ has commanded us to do so— " Do this in remembrance of me "—as you may convince yourselves by reading the Gospel of St. Luke or St. Paul's first Epistle to the Corinthians.* The Mass is the fulfilment of the prophecy of Malachias, " From the rising of the sun even to the going down thereof, my name is great among the Gentiles: and in every place there is sacrifice, and there is offered to my name a clean oblation."†

* Luke, xxii. 19; 1 Cor., ix. 24 seq.
† Malach., i. 11.

COMMUNION.

You object to the Catholic practice of giving Communion under the species of bread alone; you pretend that while giving the Body we deprive the faithful of the Blood of Christ. This is another misapprehension of our doctrine and of the truth. The Catholic Church teaches that the Body of Christ is not separated from the Blood, nor the Blood from the Body, under either species, but that Christ is living and as such present, after Consecration, under the species of both bread and wine, and is received, in communion, living and entire as He is in Heaven, under one species as well as under both. To think differently is a gross error; it supposes that Christ is still mortal, and can be present under the species, not living, but as a corpse. Christ Himself has said, "If any man eat of this bread, he shall live forever.†"

In the early ages of the Church, as history proves incontestably, communion was often given under one species only. Many grave

---

† John, vi. 52. The same in substance is repeated in verse 59.

reasons, at a later period, induced the Church to make it a universal practice for the laity. One of these reasons is, that in giving Communion under the species of wine to a large number of people, it is hardly possible to avoid irreverences; another is the scarcity of wine in many countries; but the chief motive was, that some men had arisen who taught the error that, in all cases, Communion under both species must necessarily be given to the laity.

USE OF THE LATIN LANGUAGE.

You take exception to the use of Latin in the Divine service, as it is a language which the people do not understand. The use of the Latin language is not regarded by the Church as absolutely necessary and unchangeable. In many portions of the East, she permits the use of the vernacular tongues. It was also allowed to the Sclavonians. But it does not follow from this that there are no highly important reasons for the use of the Latin.

A dead language always remains the same; it is not liable to innovations, which unsettle the old meaning of terms in living languages, or debase words that were once dignified: it secures an unchangeable precision and an unalterable dignity to our liturgy and ceremonial. Rituals and missals printed fifty or two hundred years ago, answer our purpose as well as those that come fresh from the press. If the vernacular were used, there would be a constant need of changes; in many languages, as in German for instance, it would be impossible to make use of missals and rituals printed a hundred years ago, without altering many expressions which would have become obsolete, low, or ridiculous.

The Catholic Church neither grows old nor changes; the unchangeableness of the Latin language is a type of her immutability. It is also a type of her universality and unity; it secures in her service, all the world over, the same uniformity that exists in her faith. In Asia, Africa, Australia, America, wherever a Catholic priest may travel, he finds the same missal and ritual. The Church has stamped her own character on her ceremonies: like her, they belong to all places and suit all times.

The Latin language is the better adapted to the dignity and sanctity of Divine offices, as it is placed beyond the criticism of the crowd, while the vernacular could not escape the cavils of those who pay greater attention to forms than to substance.

If the native tongue were used, it would be of little benefit to the people. In many cases it would be impracticable for the Priest to read loud enough to be understood by the whole assembly; when many Masses are said at the same time in a church, loud reading would be ridiculous and distressing; in any case it would be inconvenient for such as have already heard Mass, and wish to employ their time in other devotions. For such as desire to follow the Priest, there are translations of the whole liturgy in all the European languages.

The Latin liturgy, like all the rites and usages of the Church, has its consolations for the faithful. I once met with an American lawyer, a Protestant, who, with unusual freedom from prejudice, remarked to me that there were three things in the Catholic Church, which above all others, he liked and admired; they were the very points which for many among you, who neither examine nor reflect, are stumbling-blocks, and occasions of ridicule and accusations against us,—confession, the celibacy of our clergy, and the use of Latin in our liturgy. The reasons he gave for his preference showed a correctness of judgment which astonished me. "It must be a source of peculiar consolation for you," he said, "to be able to open your hearts to a representative of God, to receive the advice and sympathy of a friend and father, and hear the beautiful words of absolution, Thy sins are forgiven thee." He felt that celibacy is the very means best calculated to enable a Priest to fulfil his whole duty, and attend exclusively to his congregation. With regard to the use of Latin, he made the just and striking remark, that it must have a beneficial effect on the heart, and tend to enliven faith. "It must be very consoling to a Catholic," he remarked, "to hear, wherever he goes, the same language used in the Divine service as in his native country. Wherever he is, he must feel at home." In Europe I heard from some persons who had been in the suite of the Austrian Princess in her voyage to Brazil, after her marriage with Don Pedro the Emperor of Brazil, that, when they were homesick in that distant country, they found it refreshing, on entering a church, to hear the same language at the altar that had been familiar to them at home. They felt that, however remote from the land of their birth, they were still at home, as children of the same Church.

The ancient language of Rome also reminds us of the Chair of Peter, of the great center of the Church, of the imperishable rock on which the Church is founded. There cannot, indeed, be any language better adapted, in every respect, to the dignity of our service; any better calculated to console; any that reflects better the Unity, Catholicity, and Immortality of the Church of God.

CEREMONIES.

Some among you stigmatize our ceremonies as mummeries, though every intelligent man among you, and even uneducated Protestants, when they enter our churches, are involuntarily struck by the grandeur of our rites. Many Americans and large numbers of Englishmen travel to Rome, for the purpose of being present at the sublimely impressive ceremonies of Holy Week, or at the varied and magnificent religious festivals throughout the year. If any of our ceremonies really appear ridiculous and absurd, it is only to those who do not understand their signification. Before judging and condemning, it would be better to seek information on the subject: it is unworthy of an intelligent man to reject or ridicule what he does not understand.

I cannot take leave of this topic without saying a few words on a practice which I have found to be very offensive to some Protestants, and particularly so to Methodists. I refer to the Rosary or Beads. We are asked why we constantly repeat the same prayers, and are taunted as simpletons or superstitious enthusiasts for doing so.

Do you understand that which you take the liberty to blame? What is the Rosary? It consists of the most venerable prayers in existence, the Apostle's Creed, the Lord's Prayer, and the Angelic Salutation. To the Angelic Salutation we join the salutation addressed by St. Elizabeth to the Blessed Virgin, and a brief prayer added by the Church. While reciting the Rosary, we meditate on some scene or passage in the life, sufferings, death, resurrection of our Saviour, or His glorified life in heaven. Can you imagine a more beautiful form of prayer? But still you ask, Why always repeat the same prayers? And I ask you, Why not, provided the repetition contributes to devotion, and always raises our hearts to

God? Is a rose-bush less beautiful, because many roses cluster on its branches? Would it be finer with only one rose blushing in a wilderness of leaves? The Rosary takes its name from the rose: its manifold repetitions, its beautiful remembrances of the sweet mysteries of our Redemption, are like a wreath of roses grateful to God and refreshing to the soul. What if the wreath is large, and beautiful, and made up of many flowers? Must that scandalize you? Or, to use another illustration, is a mother displeased, because her favorite on her lap caressingly repeats to her, Mother, I love you, I love you dearly, Mother? Do not the hosts of the blessed, as Isaiah and St. John testify, sing night and day, Holy, holy, holy, the Lord God of Hosts? Is God injured, or the love of seraphs weakened, by the repetition? You will not pretend it. Once for all, I would commend to your reflections the advice of our Saviour, "Judge not according to the appearance, but judge a just judgment."* Learn what Catholics really hold, teach, and practice before you pass sentence upon us.

* John, viii. 24.

ABSTINENCE.

You object to the Catholic practice of fasting, and especially to our practice of abstaining from meat on Fridays and certain other days of the year. You even attempt to support your objections by quotations from Scripture; you say, "Not that which goeth into the mouth, defileth a man; but what cometh out of the mouth, this defileth a man." If your objection had any force, it would hold against the command which God gave to Adam, not to eat the fruit of a certain tree.

Abstinence is prescribed by the Church as a wholesome practice of penance, as an appropriate mode of honoring the Passion of Christ, and in imitation of His Divine example. Christ underwent voluntary suffering; it cannot be wrong to follow such a model.

Some of you, perhaps, imagine that the Church regards the use of meat as sinful in itself; this is an error. The Church knows that Christ Himself ate the paschal lamb with His disciples; she allows the use of meat at all times except on the appointed days of abstinence. But as the Church wished to establish a universal observance in honor of the Passion of Jesus Christ, and one which might at the same time be a practice of penance, what way better adapted to her purpose could she have chosen, than the prohibition on stated days of a certain kind of food? Moreover, by this precept, she affords all her children an opportunity of exercising the most necessary virtues of obedience and humility, giving a common command to all, and requiring all, the rich as well as the poor, to obey it.

EXCLUSIVE SALVATION.

You are exceedingly angry with us for asserting that out of the Catholic Church there is no salvation; you conclude that we condemn you all to everlasting ruin, before God has judged you. I reply that we teach the doctrine, and it is the truth, but your conclusion is unfounded.

The Catholic Church teaches, and has always taught, that she is the only true Church of Christ, and, therefore, that out of her pale there is no salvation: one proposition follows from the other. As soon as the Church begins to teach, which she never will, that men can be saved out of her communion, she ceases to be the true Church of Christ.

If you were at all confident that Protestantism is the true Church of Christ, you would say as much as we do, and every Religion that does not, gives up all claim to be Divinely instituted for the salvation of mankind. This I shall prove from the very idea of Religion, and, in particular, from the idea of the Christian Religion.

What is Religion? As the word implies, it is a bond which unites men to God. The idea of Religion includes faith and practice, a belief of truth and a performance of duties, by which we are to attain to the eternal possession of God, the ultimate and only end of our existence. Now, as surely as there is but one God, and but one human race, so surely can there be but one faith and one moral law, established by the Almighty to lead men to heaven.

If Religion were only a system of outward observances and external forms of worship, a mere ceremonial, then there might be as many Religions, as men might choose to frame rituals; but the question is in regard to Religion in the strict meaning of the word, and especially regarding religious faith and duties. What is truth for one is truth for all; and what is strict duty for man as such, is strict duty for every man. To deny it is to deny that God is Truth. Take Confession for instance; has it been instituted by Christ as a means of salvation, or has it not? There is no medium. If Confession has not been instituted as a means of salvation, then there is no obligation to have recourse to it; but if it has been established as a necessary means of salvation for all who have sinned after Baptism, then no one who has thus sinned can be saved without it. Are you prepared to say that God has obliged Catholics, under pain of eternal loss, to confess their sins to the Priest as His representative, but that He has not obliged Protestants to do so? The same reasoning holds good in regard to every other religious duty. In other words, if there is any Divine Religion, there can be but one, and out of it, there can be no salvation.

The reasoning so frequently resorted to, that all men have one common Father, and therefore can be saved in all Religions, is simply ridiculous. It is precisely because there is but one God that there can be but one true

Religion. Because there is but one God, the same religious duties are binding on all men, and whoever does not fulfil them must be lost forever. You say, We all believe in the same Christ. But because you all believe in the same Christ, you are all bound to accept the faith and obey the laws which He has established in His Church. His Church, as I have proved, is the Catholic Church alone, and therefore out of the Catholic Church there is no salvation. Christ has said, "If he will not hear the Church, let him be to thee as the heathen and the publican."* "He that believeth not, shall be condemned."†

If men could be saved in all Religions, there would be no necessity for the Christian Religion; Christ would have ordered His Apostles to no purpose to go and preach to all nations; His command that all men should believe, in order to be saved, would have had no meaning. If Christ has founded a Church, all that she teaches as the Church of Christ must be believed, for all her doctrines rest on the same infallible authority of Christ. To reject a single article of faith wilfully, is sufficient to incur eternal loss, for it is to deny the whole Divine character

---

* Matt., xviii. 17.
† Mark, xvi. 16.

of faith and of the Church of Christ; it is to impeach the authority and truthfulness of God. He who can neither deceive nor be deceived has revealed every article of faith taught by His Church. "Whosoever shall keep the whole law," says the Holy Ghost, "but offend in one point, is become guilty of all."* Either the whole faith is true, or the whole of it is false; we must either believe or reject the whole, for if it errs in one point, it cannot have come from God.

On the subject of exclusive salvation the doctrine of the early Fathers of the Church is unanimous. They all teach that out of the Catholic Church there is no salvation. St. Cyprian, in the middle of the third century, says in his book on the Unity of the Church, "He cannot have God for his Father, who has not the Church for his Mother." St. Augustine, who wrote at the end of the fourth and the beginning of the fifth century, says, "Whosoever is separated from this Catholic Church, shall not have life, but the anger of God remains upon him."† St. Gregory the Great, who was Pope at the end of the sixth century, thus briefly states the Catholic doctrine: "The

* James, ii. 10.
† Ad. Part. Fact. Dan. c. 141.

Holy Catholic Church teaches, that out of her communion no one can be saved."*

As Christians you believe, as well as we, that a man who dies in the state of mortal sin is lost, that " neither fornicators, nor idolaters, nor adulterers, nor the effeminate, nor sodomites, nor thieves, nor the covetous, nor drunkards, nor railers, nor extortioners, shall possess the Kingdom of God."† Is not the denial of an article of faith a mortal sin, as well as theft, drunkenness, or uncleanness? The wilful denial of an article of faith is a direct insult offered to the veracity and authority of God, and is a more grievous sin than any injury that can be inflicted upon men. There is hardly an insult which you resent more deeply than to be branded as a liar. A man may be accused of having defrauded the State, and take but little notice of the accusation, who, if he is called a liar, is ready to answer with his revolver. He who deliberately denies an article of faith calls in question the veracity of God. The man who has the boldness to say in the face of Heaven, I know that this is a revealed truth taught as such by

* Lib. Mor. 14.
† 1 Cor., vi., 9, 10.

the infallible authority of the Church of Christ, but I will not believe it; or who, when a doctrine is authoritatively proposed to him as an article of faith, does not care to inquire whether it is a revealed truth or not, that man evidently despises God as the eternal Truth, and if he dies with such an offense upon his conscience, we need not wonder that he is lost forever.

Are we, Catholics, the cause of his ruin? Do we condemn him to the pains of hell? Evidently not. He is lost by his own act; he condemns himself. When you tell us that, in spite of our being Catholics, if we die in mortal sin, we shall be lost, you are not the cause of our condemnation, you simply foretell what will happen. A bad Catholic is lost by his own fault; so when we say, that no matter how moral your lives may be, if you die in wilful heresy, you will be inevitably lost, we do not pronounce your eternal sentence, but simply warn you in time. God alone is your judge and ours; He alone can pronounce the sentence of eternal condemnation: if he condemns you for wilful unbelief, you will have incurred the sentence by your own fault, not by ours.

You may ask me, If a man is in invincible ignorance of the true faith, and yet observes the moral law, will he be lost? I answer that such a man will die in the Catholic Church. Either in his life, or at the moment of his death, the Providence of God will give him the means, extraordinary means if necessary, to know the faith, as far at least as is indispensably necessary for salvation. We must here distinguish between two classes of persons, the baptized and the unbaptized. As this is a subject but little understood, and seldom well explained, I beg your particular attention to the following remarks.

With regard to persons born in Protestant countries and validly baptized, who, from want of instruction and opportunity, have never come to the knowledge that the Catholic Church is the only true Church of Christ, if they have never committed a mortal sin, or have atoned for their sins by perfect contrition, united to a sincere desire of doing all that God may require of them, they will be saved in the ordinary way, as members of the Catholic Church. Such persons are in reality Catholics; they have entered the Church by valid baptism, and are only outwardly separated from her communion by inculpable error.

According to Catholic doctrine there is but one baptism; it is always valid, whether administered by a Christian, Jew, infidel, or heathen, provided it is conferred with the rites established by Christ and with the intention of conferring what Christ has instituted; every man who is thus baptized becomes, at the moment of his baptism, a member of the Catholic Church. It is true that Protestants are generally baptized on being received into the Catholic Church; this is done because, outside of the Catholic Church, baptism is often invalidly administered. In any case it is not our intention to confer a second baptism: we confer it conditionally, in order to give the convert the assurance that he is truly baptized. Baptism is never renewed, when no doubt exists of the validity of the first baptism. In some countries, there are large numbers of Protestants validly baptized who are invincibly ignorant of the true Church; they are members of the Catholic Church, and without knowing it die in the Catholic communion. All who are validly baptized remain Catholics, until they apostatize by a culpable adherence to an error against faith, or culpably neglect to inquire, when a well-founded suspicion of error arises in their mind. I hope that great numbers of Protestants are thus saved, not indeed as Protestants, but as members of the Catholic Church, the only true Church of Christ.

The case of heathens differs considerably from that of baptized Protestants. Heathens who are in error inculpably, and serve God to the best of their ability, according to the light which they possess, and are ready to do all that Heaven may desire from them, will certainly be saved. They may never receive the baptism of water, but for them what is called in the Catholic Church the baptism of desire, is sufficient. Their efforts to please God include the desire to know the true faith, and willingness to embrace it; and as to sanctifying grace, which is also necessary for salvation, God, who is unwilling that men should perish when they do their utmost to please Him, infuses into their souls, in the course of their lives, or at the moment of their death, the same sanctifying grace that is conferred by the baptism of water. If they fall into mortal sin, they may receive the grace to elicit an act of perfect contrition, and thereby obtain forgiveness. Their salvation is not according to the ordinary course of Providence, but the result of an extraordinary grace, conferred in view of he merits of Christ. By the baptism of desire they become members of the true Church of Christ, the Catholic Church, and are saved only as members of her communion.

In other words, there is only one way to heaven, but there are several ways that lead to the Catholic Church, for, besides the baptism of water, there is the baptism of blood, or martyrdom suffered by an unbaptized person for the faith of Christ, and the baptism of desire, of which I have just spoken. How many are saved by the baptism of desire, whether they are few or numerous, is known to God alone; we may cheerfully leave it in the hands of God, whose boundless mercy extends to every human soul, and never allows one to perish except through its own grievous fault. The Catholic Church says, with St. Thomas Aquinas, that if a man sincerely desires to know the truth, and observes the moral law to the best of his power, God, if necessary, will send an angel to enlighten him, and lead him into the Catholic Church, rather than allow him to perish. Thus we read in the Acts, that an Angel was sent to the Centurion; and it is worthy of observation that the Centurion received the Holy Ghost, and therefore became a member of the Church, before he received the baptism of water.

But you must remember that all this holds true only in regard to those who are in invincible ignorance of the true Church. It does not by any means apply to that class of persons, which I fear is very numerous who have an opportunity of knowing the truth, and wilfully neglect it; who close their eyes against the light, stifle the warnings of conscience, and, come what may, resolutely determine to die out of the Catholic Church. They do not wish to make the sacrifices which their conversion to the Catholic Church would require. They act like the Areopagites, or Felix the Roman Governor, who told St. Paul that they would hear him another time; or like the Jews who stopped their ears, and stoned St. Stephen. They cannot claim that their ignorance is invincible; they sin against the Holy Ghost, and if they die in that condition, must be lost forever.

No one who has read these pages can plead invincible ignorance. You have had an opportunity of examining, and convincing yourselves of the truth of the Catholic Church. Even if my work should not carry conviction with it, still it must have raised doubts in your minds, and it thus obliges you to pursue your researches, until you have discovered the true

Church of Christ; if you refuse to do so, you incur grievous guilt, which must cause your everlasting ruin. If you investigate with candor and perseverance, a time will come, sooner or later, when you can no longer doubt that you must embrace the Catholic faith as your only hope of salvation.

It is unjust to accuse us of a want of charity in asserting that out of the Catholic Church there is no salvation. We publish our doctrine freely, because we love you sincerely and desire your salvation. In your researches every zealous Catholic is ready to assist you. We condemn error only, and leave the judgment of consciences to God, to whom alone such judgment belongs. We love all men as children of the same Heavenly Father, and as redeemed by the same Saviour; we are ready to sacrifice for their salvation our property, our honor, our lives. The doctrine that out of the Catholic Church there is no salvation, so far from weakening our charity towards you, serves to quicken it, and to inspire us with a zeal that shrinks from no labor, no sacrifice for your salvation.

SECTION II.

POLITICAL PREJUDICES.

Having now briefly reviewed and refuted your hereditary prejudices as Protestants, I proceed to the consideration of your political prejudices, or your prejudices as American citizens.

ALLEGIANCE.

You have been taught that we owe political allegiance to the Pope, and cannot be loyal citizens. This is a calumny without a shadow of foundation in theory or practice. The Pope is for Catholics the ultimate interpreter of the moral law; when a doubt arises whether an action is morally lawful or not, the final decision rests with the Pope. From this, as is evident to every man of candor, no danger can arise to the State. The State may be imperilled, and history and experience testify that States have been brought to the verge of ruin, by the Private Interpretation of the Bible: there is imminent danger to political institutions, when men appeal to their Private Interpretation of the Bible to settle such a question, for instance, as that of Slavery.

THE INQUISITION.

The Inquisition, a word of terror, is an occasion of much prejudice against the Catholic Church. You hope that to object against us the practices of the Inquisition will act like a torch in a powder magazine, and blow up the claims, the proofs, the truth, the Divinity of the Catholic Church. We smile at the simplicity of your hopes. Every man acquainted with history, whether he is a Protestant or a Catholic, knows that the Inquisition can furnish no objection against the Church You may frighten your children with the name.

Your objections are drawn from the Spanish Inquisition. Every man who knows anything of Spanish history knows perfectly well that the Spanish Inquisition, so far as it is objectionable, is of purely political origin, and has nothing at all to do with the claims of the Catholic Church. Like the Sicilian Vespers, and the massacre of St. Bartholomew's, it was a purely political persecution against heretics and unbelievers. While it lasted, the Popes exerted their utmost efforts to control its action and prevent abuse.

But the Spanish Inquisition is not alone to blame: Protestants have had their share in the work of persecution. Whoever has studied history to any purpose, and is willing to speak impartially, must confess that the *English Inquisition* under Elizabeth was not behind the Spanish Inquisition in rigor: the only difference between the two is, that there are more numerous and more unquestionable proofs of the injustice and cruelty of the former, than of the horrors of the latter. Abuses exist in all human institutions; the Catholic Church cannot be responsible for the conduct of States and individuals which she condemns, nor for disorders which she has never commanded or approved.

If you wish to throw odium on the Church, why do you not attack the Roman Inquisition, in preference to the Spanish? The truth is, that the Roman Inquisition furnishes no fair field for calumny. It is true you often mention Galileo, but you cannot prove that he was treated cruelly. He was forbidden to teach his theory as an absolute certainty at a time when no absolute certainty existed on the subject: Galileo's proofs, as is now admitted, did not demonstrate his theory. The authority of Scripture was apparently called in question; in order to avoid scandal, Galileo was allowed to teach his theory only as an hypothesis, until it should be fully proved. His imprisonment, of which so much has been said, was nothing more than a nominal and brief confinement to the apartments of the Fiscal of the Inquisition, or to the Palace of Trinita del Monte, situated in the healthiest part of Rome. He himself wrote in 1633, that he had always been treated with respect. The story of his abjuration has not been proved, and were it proved would be a stain on his character, for the story is, that on rising after the abjuration he exclaimed, "E pur si move—It does move, though." Can you reconcile such a contradiction with his stern character?

If silence was at last imposed on Galileo, it was owing to his intemperate zeal and imprudence. At that very time his system was publicly taught at Rome as an hypothesis, without any interference from the ecclesiastical authorities. The system had warm advocates in the highest ranks of the Roman clergy. Since you place so high a value on the authority of Scripture, you must admit, that, all things considered, there was nothing in the proceedings of the Inquisition not justified by the circumstances of the time, to save the authority of the Scriptures from apparent contradiction with cosmological demonstrations. The Church has never pronounced a dogmatic definition on the subject.

The whole question of the Inquisition has nothing to do with the Church as such; it is a question of temporary and variable discipline, not a question of faith. The Church existed for ages without any such tribunal, and, with or without it, shall exist to the end of time. She is not responsible for abuses which must exist in all human institutions.

Galileo's system was censured with the utmost severity in Protestant countries. Such men as Tycho Brahe, the great Protestant astronomer, Bacon, Alexander Ross, were

opposed to it. Much, indeed, might be said about the persecution of science by Protestants. For two hundred years England refused to adopt the Gregorian Calendar, and chose "to quarrel with the stars" rather than agree with the Pope in counting time. Descartes was, in consequence of his philosophical views, most shamefully persecuted by the churchmen of Protestant Holland. Galileo was neither exiled, nor stripped of his honors and emoluments, while Christian Wolf, the most amiable of men, was wrongly accused, and condemned as an atheist by Protestants. Let Protestants, who are forever talking about the days of Galileo, remember their own Inquisitions at that very epoch. "The synod of Dort, that Protestant Council convened by Pope James, ratified its decrees in the blood of the patriot Barneveldt, and Moloch-like demanded for its victims whole hecatombs of its own children.
. . . . What Inquisition more complete than the hateful Star-Chamber? or the High-Ecclesiastical Commission-court for the suppression of heresy?" With many Protestants the story of Galileo is as fresh as though it were of yesterday, while they forget "those modes of Inquisition," as Burke said, "that should never be mentioned to ears organized

to the chaste sounds of equity and justice."*
Protestants would do better never to mention
Galileo, in order that we may not, in our turn,
be forced to inquire into their own excesses
of religious hatred.

DESPOTISM.

Your historical objections, to which the present one belongs, always turn out to be either gross misrepresentations, pure fabrications of unscrupulous writers, or irrelevant to the question whether the Catholic Church is or is not the only true Church of Christ. The question is not about individual errors and crimes—Christ did not come to make men impeccable—the question is, which is the true Church established by Christ.

Before believing what historians advance against us, you should carefully weigh their testimony. Much of what passes for history is mere fable; much of it is distorted and colored by the writers' prejudices: facts are

* See an Article on Galileo from the *Dublin Review*, republished in Cincinnati by J. P. Walsh, 1859. See also Biographie Universelle, t. IV. p. 72, and Histor. Polit. Blatter. Munich.

judged, not according to their circumstances but according to preconceived notions. This is not history, but imagination. If you love historical truth, do not believe more than historians can prove; do not confine your reading to Protestant authors alone; read the statements made by Catholic writers, and form your own judgments. If you follow this plan, your ideas regarding Catholic history will undergo considerable modifications; and though you may often find reason to condemn the acts of individual Catholics, you will never condemn the Catholic Church as such. The objection of despotism is more directly answered in a subsequent article on Republicanism.

CIVILIZATION.

You make it an objection against the Catholic Church, that Protestant nations, in your opinion, are superior to Catholic nations in industry, commerce, and general civilization. I hesitate answering an objection which is so little to the purpose; but as it is seriously urged by many among you, I shall bestow a few remarks upon it. Suppose, for the sake of argument, that things are as you represent them, what conclusion follows against the claims of the Catholic Church to be the only true Church of Christ and the only saving Church? I am astonished that such objections hould ever have been thought of. "There is no relation," as Mr. Baine justly remarks, "of cause and effect between a magnificent iron foundry and a Divine revelation, and what consequences exist in, what facts may flow from, what moral or Divine truths there may be connected with a spinning-jenny, is not perceived by the Catholic mind."*

Did Christ come to teach men the arts of commerce, to render them skilful money-makers, to train them in the construction of railroads, steamboats, and cotton factories? He has said, "My Kingdom is not of this world." "In this world you shall have distress." "What will it profit a man, if he gain the whole world, and lose his own soul?" Those who are forever making earthly success, wealth, and power a test of religious truth, are like the carnal Jews, who awaited an earthly Messiah. The blessing of Esau, "the fat of the earth," has always appeared to Christians the least desirable of all blessings; they fear

* Baine, sect. xi.

receiving their reward on earth, and having none in Heaven. If wealth and material power are signs of Divine truth, the Roman empire ought never to have forsaken its idolatry for Christianity.

The whole objection is groundless. God, because He is God, as St. Augustine remarks, can give temporal blessings to the good as well as to the wicked. France and Belgium are Catholic countries, and not behind their Protestant neighbors in civilization. Your own civilization, it must not be forgotten, is of Catholic origin. Many of your institutions are derived from Great Britain, and all that is really good, grand, and noble in the British Constitution, has come down from Catholic times. Modern civilization did not spring from Protestantism like Minerva from the head of Jove. In skill, science, art, inventions, and discoveries, Catholic nations do not yield to Protestant countries; it is an historical fact that the most important discoveries, in every branch of art, science, and industry, were in a great measure made by Catholics. Every library in the world contains immortal monuments of Catholic genius; Europe is covered with masterpieces of Catholic architects, sculptors, and painters.

What would Europe be without the civilizing influence of the Catholic Church? Little better than a wilderness, overrun by the rude descendants of Northern barbarians. The Catholic Church civilized the Huns, Goths, Lombards, Franks, Saxons, the ancestors of all the modern European nations: by the side of this immense result of Catholic influence, you cannot name a single nation reclaimed from barbarism or the savage state by Protestantism. In North America, Protestantism has not civilized a single Indian tribe; the ancient possessors of the soil of the United States have been exterminated or driven to the Western prairies. In the whole of the South, Central, and North American States, every civilized Indian tribe has received its civilization from Catholic missionaries, and their work would have been far more successful but for the frequent intrigues of Protestants. Look at Mexico, a country which you so often revile, but which would excite your admiration, did you consider the advance which it has made in civilization from the condition in which it was three hundred years ago, when inhabited by savages.

Whoever wishes to see this subject discussed

more fully, would do well to read the essays upon it in Dr. Brownson's "Quarterly Review."

MORALITY.

Many among you object, that Protestant nations are more moral than Catholic nations. This objection has been completely refuted by Dr. Brownson and other writers, and the blindest fanaticism alone could have given birth to it. So odious is it that I hesitate to give it even a cursory notice; but it has been so often brought forward, that I cannot wholly pass it over in silence.

Who has made you judges of the living and the dead? Who has revealed to you the secrets of all hearts? Or do you judge from outward appearances? Admitting that Catholic countries exhibit more outward marks of immorality, because less hypocritical, I may still ask, What follows from it as to their real moral condition, as compared with Protestant countries? Did not the Pharisees appear infinitely more holy than the Publicans? And still our Saviour calls the Pharisees "whitened sepulchres." The Publican went home justified, and the prayerful, fasting, self-righteous Pharisee is described as an arrant hypocrite. " Wo to you, Scribes and Pharisees," said our Saviour, " because you devour the houses of widows, making long prayers."* What do the crimes of individual Catholics prove? Is the Church to be condemned on their account? If so, you must condemn Christ; for one of His own Apostles betrayed Him, Peter denied Him, all fled from Him at the first sign of danger. Does the sin of the Apostles destroy their authority as Apostles and founders of the true Church of Christ, and render His Church the synagogue of Satan from the beginning? Did not the Jews crucify the Messiah? and still were they not the true Church of old?

But your objection is without foundation. It is proved by statistics that the crimes committed in England, Prussia, and the United States, exceed by far the crimes committed in Catholic countries. For proof of this fact I refer you to the report made by Dr. Forbes to the British Government, in the year 1852, in which it is shown that there is incomparably more

* Matt., xxiii. 14.

crime in London alone than in the whole of Ireland.

It is sometimes made a reproach against the Catholic Church, that there is more liveliness, more merriment, more geniality of intercourse in Catholic than in Protestant countries, and that the latter are distinguished from the former by a soberness of temper inclining to melancholy and sadness. This is a strange objection. All excess is blamable; but is cheerfulness a sin? Is it not rather a sign of moral health? Catholic nations are not made up of melancholy devotees, it is true, but that speaks in their favor. Protestants have reasons enough to be sad; we have as many reasons to be cheerful. "Rejoice in the Lord always," says the Apostle, "again I say rejoice."* I willingly admit the charge.

THE SABBATH.

You object, also, that Catholics do not keep the Sabbath or Sunday, but spend a great part of it in worldly amusements. This reproach, in some respects, and as against a certain

---
* Philip. iv. 4.

number of Catholics, is not unfounded. It is true that some Catholics break the Sabbath; but that is not the fault of the Catholic Church; she condemns their conduct as sinful. To be convinced of this, it is sufficient to open our Catechisms, or to listen to Catholic sermons. The Catholic Church, however, does not teach the rigid doctrines of Puritans and other denominations in England and America, whose views about the observance of the Sabbath are Jewish rather than Christian. The Church, in virtue of the power which she has received from Christ, abolished the Jewish Sabbath, and substituted Sunday in its stead, in commemoration of the most glorious mysteries of our Redemption. Sunday being instituted to commemorate mysteries of joy, the Church has mitigated the rigor of the Jewish Sabbath, and does not forbid as sinful, decent recreations indulged in on that day.

THE SOVEREIGNTY OF THE POPE AND HIS CIVIL GOVERNMENT.

You dislike to see the Head of the Church governing a small territory in Italy, as an independent and sovereign prince. This appears to you incompatible with his religious authority, with his duties as Head of the Church, which is a spiritual kingdom, and hence you condemn his political sovereignty.

I answer, This objection, like all other brought against the Church, arises from the lack of a thorough examination of the subject. For if you consider the Pope's situation as Head of the Catholic or universal Church, you will be forced to admit that his temporal independence as a sovereign Prince, is not only not in contradiction with his spiritual office, but on the contrary is, if not of absolute necessity, at least most expedient for the free exercise of his spiritual power. And the obvious reason is, that to enjoy the full confidence of Christians throughout the earth, he must be beyond even the suspicion of being influenced in his spiritual government by any temporal power. Were the Pope only the superintendent of a provincial Church, like the dignitaries of the Methodist, Presbyterian, and Episcopalian denominations, the case would be different. But the Pope is the Head of the whole Church in both hemispheres: the sun never sets on his Spiritual Kingdom, which unites as brethren members of all the nations on the earth. Therefore, in the ceremonies for the installation

of a new Pope, he is addressed in these words:
"Noveris te urbis et orbis constitutum esse
rectorem.—Remember that thou art placed on
the throne of Peter as the ruler of Rome and
the world." Such being his mission on earth
the freer his authority the better.

History gives us a striking proof, in the
temporary residence of the Popes at Avignon,
that even a suspicion of a preponderating
political influence is exceedingly dangerous to
the interests of religion. Every one knows
how great at that epoch were the evils that religion had to endure, simply because the freedom
of the Sovereign Pontiff seemed to be checked
by the influence of France.

Why has the District of Columbia been
rendered independent, if not because the seat
of Government being placed there, the nation
was unwilling that any particular State of the
Union, by possessing the Capitol, should have
even a shadow of preponderance in the administration of affairs. A similar reason, but with
incomparably more strength, proves the propriety of the political independence of the
Pope. Americans profess admiration for free
governments; they should therefore rejoice
that the Pope is free in the administration of
his Spiritual power.

But, besides, the dignity of the Vicar of Christ is too exalted to be borne by a subject of an earthly prince. Such seems to have been the pervading sentiment of Christian princes since the days of Constantine the Great. This great Emperor, who first placed the cross on his crown, transferred his residence to Constantinople, and, what is still more remarkable in this connection, even after the division of the Roman Empire, none of the Western Emperors resided in Rome, but in Milan, Turin, or other places.

As to the pretended abuses of the Papal government, I have only to say that the source whence you derive your information, is sufficient to cause its rejection. You rely almost exclusively on the accounts of them given by Englishmen, who, influenced by the fanatical tendencies of their country, endeavor by misrepresentation and exaggeration to inflame public opinion against the Pontifical administration. A similar spirit of fanaticism too often pervades newspapers, books of travel, and other publications in this country.

Candid inquiry proves that there are fewer defects in the administration of the Papal States than in that of any other State, Empire, or Republic. The very last statistics demonstrate, beyond a doubt, that with respect to schools, benevolent institutions, and the proper administration of the laws, the States of the Church are rather in advance of every other country. This has been shown conclusively by several works lately published, amongst others by Mr. Maguire's work on "Rome, its Churches, its Charities, and its Institutions," to which I refer you for fuller information on this matter.

REPUBLICANISM.

The last objection I shall notice is that, as some among you contend, the Catholic Church is not in harmony with the institutions of this country, nor with the character of its people, and that she is generally opposed to liberal political institutions.

The truth is the very reverse of the objection. Though the government of the Catholic Church is not properly republican, yet all the blessings which render your form of government dear to you, are claimed by the Catholic Church as peculiarly belonging to her own form of government; and your national character, if the country should become Catholic, would make you as good and zealous Catholics, under Divine grace, as exist on earth. I will briefly prove these assertions.

The soul of your political institutions is liberty. Liberty is all the Catholic Church demands for herself; she needs not, and does not ask, any special protection; give her the full freedom guaranteed her by the Constitution, and enjoyed by every sect of Christians, and she is satisfied. The sun does not ask light from the earth; her own beams disperse the morning fog, and pierce the cloud. All the Church demands for her prosperity and growth, all she needs to remove your prejudices, is freedom of action.

Gregory XVI. used to say, "Out of the Roman States, there is no country where I am Pope, except the United States." In Catholic countries, as the numerous Concordats prove, the Church in many respects has her rights restricted; here she is legally free, the only Concordat she asks is your Constitution. Indeed, all she asks in any country is her freedom, not Concordats; she has no need of Concordats when she is free.

Under your Constitution the ablest men, without respect to birth or ancestry, are chosen for public offices. The same practice prevails in the Church. Run over any list of Popes, Cardinals, or Bishops, and you will find that most of them sprang from the common people; those descended from the nobility almost form the exception. Never has a single king or prince sat on the Papal chair. According to the laws of the Church, talent, virtue, merit, are the qualities by which the appointment or election to ecclesiastical offices must be guided, and these qualities exercise a more uniform and decided influence in the Church, than they do even in the American republic. You have a striking proof of this in the person of Gregory VII., in whom, according to Protestant estimation, all the power of the Popes was concentrated as in a focus: he was the son of a carpenter. The avenue to the Papacy is open to every Catholic; even a layman may become a Pope, and I was informed by Cardinal Spinola that the practice at this day, when a new Pope is to be elected, is to place a lay senator on the list of candidates.

Prejudiced and partial historians, who shape facts to suit their preconceived opinions and preferences, are in the habit of calumniating the Catholic hierarchy, and especially the olitical conduct of the Popes. They may impose on the ignorant multitude, but cannot deceive the impartial researches of the learned. The Popes who have been most reviled have found defenders in the ranks of Protestants; Gregory VII. has been vindicated in the beautiful history of his reign by the Protestant Voit and Innocent III. in the great work of Hurter, written while he was still a Protestant. The stereotype slanders against them have been refuted, and they have taken their place before the world among the brightest ornaments of history. "There is no line of men," says the learned Protestant historian Herder, "so distinguished for talent and for virtue, as the magnificent succession of the Popes." Among the Roman Pontiffs, hardly five or six, in eighteen centuries, can be named in whom the implacable hostility of the enemies of the Catholic Church, has been able to find a stain; and nearly all these few are limited to the eleventh century, an unruly period, when the freedom of Papal elections was disturbed by external interference. And what, after all, are these few Popes reproached with? Herder will answer, "Their faults were such as would not have been noticed, had they not been the moral failings of the Popes; they are such as would pass unnoticed in other princes."

It is an undeniable fact, if anything in history is undeniable, that none have labored more successfully for the freedom of nations than the Popes, as is proved by their undying struggle against oriental and occidental despots. This glorious fact is acknowledged by Protestant historians, and even by such men as Montesquieu and the unprincipled Voltaire, not one of whom can be suspected of any partiality towards the Roman See. Leo, Wolfgang Menzel, and other great modern Protestant historians, admire with us the strenuous efforts of the Papacy in behalf of freedom. At this hour, almost alone in Europe, in the face of high-handed oppression, and hypocritical professions of love for freedom, it holds up before the nations its time-honored banner of genuine freedom. You know the efforts of Pius IX. and why he failed.

FREEDOM OF DISCUSSION.

You love liberty of speech; the Catholic Church loves it no less. "*In necessariis unitas, in dubiis libertas*—Unity in things necessary, freedom in doubtful ones," is one of her oldest and most celebrated maxims. The Pope decides no point of importance without first submitting it to the discussion of the Cardinals and men of learning. In Councils and Synods the greatest freedom of speech prevails. At all times every Catholic is free to appeal from the decision of subordinate authorities to the Holy See. Freedom of discussion is not, as you imagine, condemned by the Catholic Church.

Mr. Baine very effectually refutes the charge that the Catholic Church is opposed to free institutions in general, and especially to the Constitution of this country. Appealing to the evidence of historical facts, he says, " We affirm, whenever the rights and liberties of any people, for fifteen hundred years, have been in jeopardy, by tyranny from any quarter where the Church has had any influence, that she and her children have exerted that influence on behalf of the oppressed and down-trodden, and in favor of liberty and against tyranny. We affirm more, and further, that the noblest charter of human rights that the world has ever seen wrested from tyranny and feudal institutions, within eighteen hundred years, was forced from a despot by the genius, courage, and learning of Catholics, under the auspices and encouragement of their spiritual

Mother, the Church. And what is more still every principle of liberty in the American Constitution, which is declaratory of, and which conserves the liberties of the American people, is a literal transcript in substance, and almost in terms, from that Catholic charter of human rights of which we now speak. Every American school-boy is familiar with the old renown of 'Magna Charta,' wrung from King John by barons of England. But if American Protestant school-boys were informed that these sturdy barons, who evinced so much pertinacious courage, and political genius, and profound insight into the principles on which civil liberty depends, and upon which it now lives in the United States, were every one of them Catholics, these same boys would stare at you in blank amazement. They have been taught to reverence Magna Charta, and to denounce the Church as inimical to civil liberty, in the same breath. The same school-boy exercise that applauds the one to the skies, denounces the other to the pit. A great wrong has been done, is doing, to the understanding and hearts of these youths, who are the men of tomorrow."*

* Baine, p. 247.

The history of the Catholic Church in all ages proves to evidence that she is with the people; she lives, has always lived, in the very midst of the people. She is, and has always been, at home in all nations; she sanctions all legitimate forms of government. Since the day of Pentecost, there has been no language which has not been the vernacular tongue of her children; no form of civil institutions under which her children have not lived.

If the accusation that the Catholic Church is hostile to civil freedom is founded on historical facts, nothing can be easier than to specify in what age, in what nation, under what circumstances, the Catholic Church has destroyed human liberty or democratic forms of government. History disproves the charge. There is a little Republic in Italy, San Marino, the oldest Republic now existing, and the most unflinching and uncompromising advocate of democratic principles: that republic, which has enjoyed its independence for thirteen hundred years, is and has always been Catholic, and has been for centuries under the protection of the Pope.

The Catholic Church is not hostile to your free and glorious institutions. You have nothing to fear from her. Nothing but misrepresentation of her doctrine and discipline, could ever have engendered the belief that she wishes to undermine the republic.

One beneficial result of the late Know-Nothing movement, which originated partly in a desire to injure the Catholic Religion, has been to draw the attention of many earnest American Protestants to our doctrines; and the consequence has invariably been a favorable opinion of the Catholic Church, and, in some cases, conversion to the Catholic faith. I may mention, as an instance, the conversion of the son of a Protestant minister at Toledo. Being present at a meeting-house on an occasion when the minister indulged in a violent invective against the Catholic Church, and represented her as the mother of abominations and a sink of reprobation, the young man felt convinced that the preacher was slandering her, and he resolved to discover the truth. He read, examined, compared, and the result was that he became a Catholic. His father, I learned, became a Catholic before him.

It is a remarkable fact that Americans, when converted to the Catholic Church, are generally among the most decided and practical Catholics. I heard this on my first arrival in America from a friend who had been long in the country and knew it well, and my experience has convinced me of the correctness of his observations. Americans do not become nominal Catholics; if they have become converts at all, they are men of action and resolute will, setting a bright example of active and energetic faith to their fellow-Catholics. In view of this undeniable fact, a Roman journal, some time ago, expressed the opinion, that one of the most glorious enterprises for the Catholic Church to engage in at this day, is the conversion of the United States to the Catholic faith. If these pages contribute ever so little towards the accomplishment of the glorious undertaking, I shall be amply rewarded for my humble share in the labor.

There are many among you who regard a change of religion as dishonorable and morally wrong. This is the most dangerous of all prejudices, and the most unfounded. It cannot be dishonorable to renounce error for truth, to pass from a false Religion to the true one; it cannot be wrong to fulfil the most important duty of man, that of rendering public testimony to the truth, and to serve God as He desires to be served. To renounce a false Religion and profess the true one, is the most honorable act you can perform. By leaving the sect in which you were born to become a member of the true Church, when you have become convinced of the validity of her claims, you give to God the honor which He has a strict right to require of you, for you simply confess that God is Truth and can have revealed only one Religion; you honor Christ, for you solemnly acknowledge before the world that the only true Church is the Church founded by Him, and preached by His Apostles; you honor the Church of Christ, because, in the face of public prejudice, and perhaps of persecution, you recognize her as His Church; you honor your own understanding and heart, for you assert your independence, and trample under foot the ignominious principle that every one should remain in the Religion in which he happens to have been born, whether that Religion is true or false.

It is astonishing that the principle, that every one ought to remain in his own Religion, should ever have been accepted or advanced. On all other subjects a widely different principle is the general rule of human conduct; men universally aim at the best. Is Religion so worthless that we need not care whether it is true or false? No greater recklessness can be imagined than indifference to the question of the truth or falsehood of Religion. The question is inseparably connected with salvation; Religion, in its very nature, is the only way of salvation, and, as I have shown, there can be but one true Religion, but one which can lead a man to heaven.

What would you say of a traveler who goes South when his destination is North, and refuses to retrace his steps after he has discovered his error; and who in spite of guide-posts and positive information from persons thoroughly acquainted with the country, keeps on in the wrong direction, consoling himself with the idea that one road is as good as another? Is his conduct reasonable, especially if the future happiness of his whole life depend upon his journey?

If a man born blind and lame could be cured, we should think him mad were he to say to the physician, I should like well enough to be cured, but then I was born as I am, and my father was blind and lame as well as I; I will not take the trouble requisite for my cure. It would be madness in a sick person to be satisfied with any medicine, simply because it is a medicine. A physician died, leaving a large number of recipes. The heir, who had never studied medicine, hung out his signboard as a physician. When applied to, he used to take out at random and copy one of the recipes in his possession, and give it with the remark that it must be a very good prescription, for it had been left him by an eminent physician. The man who believes every religious quack that sets up a new Religion, is as reckless and mad as any of the madmen I have described.

If the principle that every one should remain in his own Religion is sound, why did Christ establish His Church and send His Apostles to convert the nations? If your reasoning holds good, the Jews and the Gentiles had a right to reject the new Religion, and say that they wished to retain their old one; Christianity could never have been propagated, and we should be heathens at the present day.

The principle is wrong. Whoever discovers that he is in a false Religion, is bound to abandon it for the true. By doing so, he only fulfils an essential duty, the first and most important of all the duties which thé creature owes to his Creator, the duty of submitting to the will of God without regard to inconvenience, affliction, or persecution.

Some among you who have received Confirmation in Protestant sects, are greatly disturbed at the thought of a change of Religion, looking upon it as a culpable breach of the oath they have taken to remain Protestants. Their fears are groundless; unlawful oaths are not binding. No one will say that Herod was obliged by his oath to give the head of John the Baptist to the daughter of Herodias. God cannot accept an oath which is contrary to truth or justice. Were you to take an oath to deliver your soul up to Satan, do you think the oath would be binding? Can you oblige yourself by oath to resist the inspirations of the Holy Ghost and reject the truth? The oath taken at a Protestant Confirmation, if it has any force, obliges you to become Catholics. If it has any lawful meaning, it means that you bind yourself to remain a Protestant only because you believe Protestantism to be true Christianity; therefore if you discover that the Catholic Church is the only true Church, and that you cannot be a true Christian except by becoming a Catholic, your oath, if binding, obliges you to become a member of the Catholic Church. Suppose you had taken an oath to regard a bank bill as genuine and to pass it as such, would you be obliged to keep your oath, if, on attempting to pass the note, you discover that it is counterfeit? Would you not be glad to exchange it for a good one, if any one should, of his own accord, make the offer? You ought to be exceedingly thankful to God for having discovered the falsehood of Protestantism, and being able to leave it for the true Church.

To become a Catholic is simply to return to the truth from which Luther departed. A convert from Protestantism, if asked why he changed his Religion and became a Catholic, may answer that he did so because Luther himself was a Catholic; he may say, Ask Luther why he changed, I have only returned to the truth. This was Count Stolberg's answer to the King of Prussia, who had remarked to him, that he did not like people who changed their Religion. "Neither do I like them, sire," was the reply; "If Luther had not changed, I should have had no occasion to do what I have done; I have only returned to the first Church." "It is a shame," says St. Augustine, "to change one's opinion if it is right and true, but to change a false and dangerous opinion is praiseworthy and useful. As fortitude does not allow a man to become depraved, so obstinacy does not allow him to amend: as the former is praiseworthy, so the latter should be corrected."*

One great obstacle to conversion is public opinion. To become a Catholic is simply to perform a duty on which happiness in time and eternity depends; yet hundreds who are convinced that the Catholic Church is the only true Church of Christ, are prevented by fear of censure from following their convictions. They fear displeasing their relations; they dread the opinion of the world, and choose to please men, rather than obey God. They choose to incur the dreadful denunciations of Christ: "Whosoever shall confess me before men, I will also confess him before my Father, who is in heaven. But whosoever shall deny me before men, I will also deny him before my Father, who is in heaven. . . . . He that loveth father or mother more than me, is not worthy of me; and he that loveth son or daughter more than me, is not worthy of me."† They determine to expose themselves to the eternal anger of God, sooner than incur the displeasure or censure of men. The fear of blame is the rock on which the noblest hearts have suffered eternal shipwreck.

* St. Aug. Epist. ad Celer.
† Matt., x. 32. seq.

Why should you fear taking a step for which you can assign the best of reasons? Why should you fear the opinion of men, particularly in this country? You boast of freedom of conscience and Religion; but what sort of freedom is that which prevents you from following your convictions, and holds you enchained in the fetters of education, habit, and public opinion? Liberty, if it is worth anything, ought to make you bold enough to acknowledge no judge of conscience except God.

So far I have addressed Protestants; but a great number of Americans profess no Religion whatever, and are simply infidels. I have to address them also, not only because I am persuaded that many of them are not hostile to the truth if it is once clearly presented to them, but also because the order of my argument leads me to the discussion of Infidelity, as it is the ultimate consequence of Protestantism.

CHAPTER IV.

INFIDELITY;
OR, THE ULTIMATE CONSEQUENCE OF PROTESTANTISM.

I CALL Infidelity the last logical consequence of Protestantism, and I have a right to do so. There are Infidels in Catholic countries, but they are not Infidels in consequence of the Catholic Rule of Faith; Infidelity cannot be deduced from the principle of infallible authority in matters of Faith. But Protestantism by asserting the Private Interpretation of the Bible as the only Rule of Faith, renders faith impossible, and gives a clear right to believe nothing that is beyond the sphere of natural truth, since no certainty in relation to supernatural truth can be arrived at by the Private Interpretation of the Bible.

The remarks which I have to make in this chapter, are addressed to Infidels, no matter whence or how their Infidelity may have arisen; if they will only read and reflect for a single hour, they will be forced to acknowledge that Infidelity is self-contradictory. My reasoning shall be brief, as the nature of a popular discussion demands, but it will be conclusive. However, I address myself to those only who are acquainted with history, and capable of following a course of logical reasoning.

I will place before you seven conclusive arguments, each of them so conclusive, indeed, that you must either admit them all in succession, and thus be led to recognize the infallible authority of the Catholic Church, or be at war with reason.

SECTION I.

INFIDELITY REFUTED.

FIRST CONCLUSIVE ARGUMENT.

THE UNDENIABLE EXISTENCE OF GOD.

There is a God, this is the first in the series of truths to be proved to Infidels. There is a God; to deny it, is to contradict human reason. If you look at this world, not like a dumb animal, but with the eye of reason, you must confess that there is a God. If there is no God, how did the world originate? If you deny the existence of God, you must say, either that nothing produced the world out of nothing, or that it has existed from eternity; but either assertion clearly involves a contradiction

To say that nothing produced the world out of nothing, is not only absurd, but too ludicrous to call for a serious refutation. Where nothing acts upon nothing, nothing must be the result for all eternity.

Father Kircher, the celebrated Roman astronomer and philosopher, had a friend who was a thorough-going Infidel, but admired him for his genius and learning. Father Kircher one day showed him a beautiful miniature globe. "Who made it?" inquired the Infidel. "Why," answered Father Kircher, "nobody made it. Last night it came into existence out of nothing, and I found it in my room this morning." "Do you mean to make a fool of me?" asked his friend, not a little nettled. "Then you believe," said the father, "that no one but a fool could imagine that this globe came into existence out of nothing of its own accord; and yet you believe that the whole universe, of which this little globe is but a small representation, started into being without a Creator. Is not this idea a thousand times more extravagant than the other?"

"You cannot find a hut in the woods," says Cicero, "without concluding that some one was there to build it; and you look at this universe, its grandeur, and harmony, and yet pretend that no one made it!"

If you say that there is no need of a Creator because the world has existed from eternity you fall into an absurdity no less glaring. Wherever there is number, there can be no infinity, for numbers can always be increased; and where there is no infinity, there must be a beginning, and consequently no eternity. But there is number in the world; everything in it is changeable; every object in it is in motion; and changes and motions may be computed or numbered. To-day is a day added to yesterday. If the world were eternal, days would have existed from eternity, these would be an infinite number, which is a palpable absurdity, for to any number we can always add unity. Days cannot have existed without a first day, in the same manner that a chain cannot exist without a first link: an infinite number of days, is as absurd as a chain with an infinite number of links, and no first link. As certain as it is that to-day is a day more than yesterday, and that time is time, so certain it is that the world had a beginning, that there is a Creator, who is eternal, that there is a God.

SECOND CONCLUSIVE ARGUMENT.

THE UNDENIABLE IMMORTALITY OF THE SOUL.

The immortality of the soul, is as certain as the existence of God. Our existence had a beginning, but it will have no end; eternity awaits us. To assert the contrary involves a contradiction.

Our immortality is as certain as God's existence. God is free; He could create me, or not create me, as He pleased, but having created me a reasonable being, he could not have created my soul mortal. To create a reasonable soul mortal, would be in contradiction to His justice and goodness, and to the nature of a spiritual being such as the human soul; and being in contradiction to the justice and goodness of God, it implies a denial of his existence, for His existence is essential justice and goodness.

God has created me either for happiness or misery; if for misery, He is cruel, and I am not bound to return thanks to Him for my creation. If He has created me for happiness, and yet deprives me of it without any fault of mine, by annihilating my soul, then His cruelty is still greater, and I am still less obliged to thank Him. There is no greater misfortune, as Cicero has remarked, than to be in the enjoyment of happiness and to know that it will soon be over. The greater the happiness, the more painful is the loss of it; the greater the bliss which a man enjoys, and the longer the enjoyment lasts, the greater would be his misery were he to discover that he is to be annihilated. He might justly say to his Creator, Thou hast made me, and made me happy; why dost thou deprive me of my existence? I do not thank thee for having created me; infinitely better had it been for me never to have existed, than to have been created for annihilation. Such language is blasphemy, and still, were our souls not immortal, it would be just.

I do not speak here of those who offend God mortally, and thus incur eternal punishment through their own fault; I only argue against those who assert that the soul is not immortal, and yet grant that it is capable of happiness. God cannot annihilate the human soul, because He cannot contradict Himself.

To say that the soul is mortal, is in contradiction likewise to the nature of a spiritual being. A spirit has no parts, a body is composed of parts: if the soul were a material substance, it might be destroyed, for all material substances can be dissolved; but being a spirit, it is incapable of dissolution, it can only be annihilated. Only infinite Power can annihilate a being, for the same power is required for annihilation as for creation, and only infinite Power can create, or call forth creatures out of nothing. God will not annihilate the human soul, for, as I have shown, to annihilate it would contradict His infinite perfections.

To say that the soul is a material substance or body, is absurd and ridiculous. The soul is a thinking principle; thought is its effect. There can be no effect without an adequate cause; the effect cannot be greater than the cause, nor of a nature opposite to the cause. If the soul is a material substance, there would exist an effect of a higher nature than the cause, for the soul, the thinking principle, would be essentially inferior to its effect, thought; thought is immaterial, while the soul would be material. Thought, as every one is conscious, is a simple act; therefore the principle of thought, the soul, must be simple. If the soul is material, the thinking principle and its effect are of opposite natures, which clearly involves a contradiction.

As this reasoning may be too metaphysical for some of my readers, I shall endeavor to put it in a more intelligible form. Bodies have shape, color, weight, size: if the soul is a material substance, its thoughts, wishes, affections, must be of the same nature, and have the same properties as bodies; but to assign measure, weight, color, shape to thoughts, is so ridiculous, that no materialist could attempt to do so, without bursting into a laugh at his own folly. I ask you, boldest of materialists, can you imagine a thought weighing a pound or an ounce; a thought a foot or half a foot in length or thickness; a yellow, orange, or red thought; a square, round, or triangular thought; a thought that smells like the rose, or has the sound of brass? The theory of materialists is ridiculous.

If the soul is not material, it cannot die; it can only be annihilated; but annihilation is an act of God's omnipotence, and God cannot exert His power in contradiction to His infinite goodness and justice. The immortality of the soul, therefore, is as certain as the existence of God, as certain as the existence of human reason.

THIRD CONCLUSIVE ARGUMENT.

THE UNDENIABLE NECESSITY OF RELIGION.

If there is a God and we are immortal, then there must be a Religion; to say the contrary implies a contradiction. The existence of God, our reason, and immortality, are necessarily the foundation of duties, on the fulfilment or non-fulfilment of which our eternal destiny depends; this is Religion. Whatever God creates, He creates for an end; else he would act without Wisdom, and would not be God; therefore man is created for an end. Every object in the universe has its laws; therefore man has laws, which bind his will, and by which he must regulate his conduct, in order to attain the end for which he is created. Those laws constitute Religion: Religion is the bond that unites us to God as our Creator and Lord; it embodies truths to be believed, and duties to be performed; it is as certain as God's existence, as certain as our reason and free-will.

FOURTH CONCLUSIVE ARGUMENT.

THE UNDENIABLE NECESSITY OF REVELATION.

With the question of Religion, arises the question whether man needs a Revelation. Can man discover the truths and duties of Religion by the unaided light of reason? or does he stand in need of a Divine Revelation for the purpose? That there is a Religion is self-evident; that we owe certain duties to God, and that those duties have a connection with our future destiny, clearly follows from the first principles of reason. But is it enough for us to know and practise only what we can discover by the light of reason without any *supernatural* Revelation? Is man, without the aid of Revelation, able to answer satisfactorily the fundamental questions, What is God? Whence do we come? What will be our destiny hereafter? What becomes of the soul after death? What is the origin of moral evil, and of our inclination to evil? When man has sinned, does there remain for him any hope of salvation, and on what conditions? What does

God demand of us, as a necessary condition of our eternal happiness? I ask, Is it possible for reason, unenlightened by Revelation, to give to these questions, a distinct, precise, complete, and unnerring answer? Every man's consciousness and the experience of all ages show that it is impossible.

With regard to the nature of God, there is no doubt, that in all times and places, men could by the light of reason alone, come to the knowledge of God. As a matter of fact, however, they did not generally rise to that knowledge. Every one knows how erroneous were the ideas men had of the Deity during the long ages which preceded the coming of Christ, and what wrong ideas are still entertained on this point among the tribes and nations that have not as yet received the light of the Gospel. But even supposing that all men did recognize God as God, still, what could they or did they know, by human reason alone, of their relation to Him, of their future destiny, or of the other questions to which I have referred? On those questions reason either is silent, or gives a doubtful, unsatisfactory answer. Yet to all those fundamental questions man has a right to ask a clear and satisfactory answer; that right is

given him by the wisdom and justice of God
He has no right to prescribe the manner in
which God should manifest His will; he has
no right to demand a supernatural destiny
but he has an inalienable right to know his
destiny whatever it may be, and to have the
means of attaining it placed within his reach.
There are now a thousand millions of men in
the world, God's creatures, every one of whom
has a right to ask, and insist on being answered,
why he is on this earth ; what God requires of
him ; what destiny awaits him in another
world ; what he must do to expiate his sins ;
what he must do, in order to secure his eternal
felicity. There is not a man on earth, capable
of reflection, who can find any real repose of
mind or heart, until these questions are distinctly and fully answered: not to desire an
answer, is to place one's self in opposition to
the most urgent requirements of reason.

On those questions reason alone can give no
clear answer. To be convinced of this, propose the questions to an Infidel, who takes
reason alone for his guide. He cannot solve
them, nor give a single satisfactory answer
His own desire to penetrate the mystery that
enshrouds the future world, is so irresistible,
that it leads him to evoke the dead, and give

credit to the revelations of Table-Turning and Spirit-Rapping. This alone is enough to show that the longing to be acquainted with the mysteries of another life, exercises so complete an empire over the soul, that rather than not know anything about them, man is ready to believe in false or diabolical revelations.

FIFTH CONCLUSIVE ARGUMENT.

THE UNDENIABLY DIVINE MISSION OF CHRIST.

Man has a right to inquire whether God has actually made a Revelation. Whether Revelation is necessary or not, it is certain that man has a right to ask whether there exists a Divine Revelation; whether God has spoken to men, or sent a messenger from heaven to reveal His will, to explain the mysteries of our destiny, to instruct us in our duties, and acquaint us with the conditions on which our eternal happiness depends.

To the question, whether God has made a Revelation, history answers that He has done so; that for many ages, at different periods, there arose men who claimed to have received a Divine Revelation, and to teach a Divinely revealed Religion. The Egyptian Priests, the Persian Zoroaster, Numa Pompilius, Confucius, Mahomet, and others, pretended that their Religion was revealed. Moses proclaimed that God himself had given him the Law; the Jewish prophets foretold the future in the name of God : their mission was preparatory to that of Christ. Christ proclaimed Himself the Son of God, and that the Father had sent Him to teach mankind the Divine Will.

I suppose you are sufficiently acquainted with history to know, that the ancient Egyptian, Roman, Persian, and Chinese founders of Religions, never proved the validity of their mission. It is not so with Christ.

The whole argument for the Divinity of the Mission of Christ, turns on this single question Was Christ in reality what He proclaimed himself to be?

In our times Infidels such as Strauss, Feuerbach, and their disciples, have labored hard and long to show that Christ was not even an historical personage, but a mere myth. They have labored in vain. God has placed the evidences of the existence of Christ, of His Mission and His miracles, beyond the reach of successful attack. The historical existence of

Christ is testified to in all ages by His hereditary enemies, the Jews. Divine Providence has allowed the ancient Persians, Egyptians, Romans to disappear from the face of the earth; but the Jews, the weakest of all the ancient nations, have survived the wreck of all the empires of antiquity, and will survive to the end of time. In vain, while they exist, does the sophist argue against the existence of Christ: by their presence in all ages, by their dispersion over all countries, the Jews are witnesses easily appealed to, and whose testimony is conclusive against him. They hold in their hands the prophecies describing His coming, His life, His sufferings, ages before His appearance on earth. The existence of the Jews is a living monument of His existence, their hatred an invincible proof of the historical truth of Christianity. While the Jews exist, and the Old Testament is in their hands, the Infidel has no hope of success; they meet him everywhere, and destroy the laborious fabric of his fallacies by the disinterested testimony of their hatred. Their anxiety for the genuineness of the Old Testament, renders interpolation or corruption of the text impossible; they have counted its letters, they can tell how often each letter occurs, and which is the first, middle one, and last.

In the prophetic books of the Jews we have, as Bossuet remarks, the history of Christ as clearly related as in the Gospels. The prophecy of Daniel, for instance, describes the precise time of His coming, foretells His rejection by the Jews, the destruction of the Temple and the city; it is so decisive that the Rabbis have pronounced a curse on the Jew who should attempt to explain it. The Jews are not only unimpeachable witnesses of the genuineness of the prophecies; their jealousy is an evident proof of the prophecies that relate to Christ. The Jews place the historical existence of Christ beyond the possibility of doubt.

An Infidel once told me, that having had the curiosity to visit a Synagogue, his attention was arrested by the tablets of the law displayed on the wall. "I shuddered at the sight," he said, "and I asked myself, What if all that is taught by the Catholic Church were true?" The whole series of ancient prophecies must have flashed across his mind, together with their obvious accomplishment in Christ. If the prophecies inspire you with fear, it is your own fault: believe, and the promises of faith, instead of terrifying you, will be your greatest consolation.

The Divine Mission of Christ is evident, not only from the prophecies, but from His own *professions*, confirmed by His life, His doctrine, His miracles, and particularly by the miracle of His Resurrection: from all these the Divinity of His Mission is as clear as the sun at mid-day.

The Divinity of His Mission is evident from His own professions. "This is life everlasting," He said, "that they may know Thee, the only true God, and Jesus Christ, whom Thou hast sent."* The Samaritan woman said to Jesus, "I know that the Messias cometh (who is called Christ); therefore when He is come, He will tell us all things. Jesus saith to her: I am He, who am speaking with thee."† Christ affirms that He is the Messiah, the Son of God, the One sent for our Redemption; He affirms it in the presence of His Apostles: "Jesus saith to them: But whom do you say that I am? Simon Peter answering said: Thou art Christ the Son of the living God."

---

* John, xvii. 3.
† John, iv. 25, 26.
‡ Matt., xvi. 15, 16.

Christ did not deny it, but confirmed him in His belief: "Blessed art thou, Simon Bar-Jona: because flesh and blood have not revealed it to thee, but my Father who is in heaven. And I say to thee: That thou art Peter, and upon this rock I will build my Church; and the gates of hell shall not prevail against it."* Christ made the same professions in public. He asked the man who had been born blind, "Dost thou believe in the Son of God? He answered and said: Who is He, Lord, that I may believe in Him? And Jesus said to him: Thou hast both seen Him, and it is He who talketh with thee. And he said: I believe, Lord. And falling down he adored Him."† Christ permitted the adoration. He made the same professions in presence of His deadly enemies: "Amen, amen, I say to you, before Abraham was made, I am."‡ "I and the Father are one."§ "He that seeth me, seeth Him that sent me."|| When Jesus had said, "I and the Father are one," "the Jews took up stones to stone Him. Jesus answered

---

* Ibid. 17, 18.
† John, ix. 35. seq.
‡ John, viii. 58.
§ John, x. 30.
|| John, xii. 45.

them: Many good works I have shown to you from the Father: for which of those works do you stone me? The Jews answered Him: For a good work we stone thee not, but for blasphemy: and because that Thou, being a man, makest Thyself God. Jesus answered them . . . If I do not the works of my Father, believe me not. But if I do, though you will not believe me, believe the works, that you may know and believe that the Father is in me, and I in the Father."*

Taking these professions in connection with the whole history of Christ, we find them proved by His life, His doctrine, His miracles, His death, His Resurrection.

1. THE LIFE OF CHRIST.—Christ could say before His enemies, " Which of you shall convince me of sin ?"† and no one came forward to prove a single accusation against Him. Among the most violent enemies of Christianity that have ever existed, hardly a single one has been bold enough to bring a charge against the character of Christ. If any have accused Him, they were of that class of reckless blasphemers who directed their insults

* John, x. 30-38.
† John, viii. 46

against God Himself. Even Voltaire and Rousseau admired the wonderful greatness of the virtues of Christ; Rousseau confessed that if the death of Socrates was that of a wise man, the death of Christ was that of a God.

It is the fashion of modern Infidels to place Christ amongst the greatest and wisest of mankind, and to call Him a hero of virtue. But in doing so they contradict themselves. Jesus is either what He claimed to be, true God and true Man, or else He was the greatest impostor the world has ever seen, and you have no right to call Him a great, wise, or virtuous man. If Christ was not the true Son of God, sent by the Father for the redemption of the world; then, as Lessing has justly remarked, Mahomet himself has not deceived the world half as much as He, and is a far better man. Mahomet only claimed to be a prophet, a man invested with extraordinary powers; Christ proclaimed Himself to be God, and allowed Himself to be adored. A mere man who pretends to be God, and permits himself to be adored, and leads millions of men into idolatry age after age, has no claim to be called wise or virtuous. To imagine one's self a God, is madness; to demand universal adoration, without any title to it, stamps the man who attempts it, if he is not insane, as the vilest impostor and the greatest malefactor that can be conceived. Christ is either truly God, or you have to say that He is the worst of men.

2. THE DOCTRINE OF CHRIST is in harmony with the Divine Mission which He claimed to have received. "Never," said the Jews, "did man speak like this man."* Centuries have gone by since then, and it is still true that no man has ever spoken as He spoke. Read the Gospels. I do not here urge them as inspired, but only as historical records of the actions and doctrine of Christ, and as worthy of credit as the most faithful of ancient or modern annals. Is not the doctrine which is inculcated in the Gospel, though constituting but a portion of the teachings of Christ, such as we might expect from a messenger of Heaven? Men could never have invented it. You cannot name a book, unless its contents be derived from the Gospels, which instructs in so authoritative a manner, and imparts instruction so pure and holy; none that, however frequently it may be read, retains so well its

---

* John, vii. 46.

original freshness, and its primitive impress of superhuman sanctity. The doctrine of the Gospels bears the stamp of its origin, the seal of its Divine author; it is always new, it is unalterable like God from whom it came Other works weary by repeated perusal; the Gospels are always interesting, always invigorating to the soul, always brilliant and spotless like the sun.

3. MIRACLES OF CHRIST.—The Divine Mission and the doctrine of Christ are confirmed by an infinite number of miracles. Jesus was able to say to the disciples of John the Baptist, "Go and relate to John what you have heard and seen. The blind see, the lame walk, the lepers are cleansed, the deaf hear, the dead rise again."* Christ appeals to His miracles in presence of His enemies, before whom He had wrought them, and who could not deny them, and did not attempt to deny them. The chief Priests and Pharisees said, "What do we, for this man doeth many miracles?"† They said so on occasion of the raising of Lazarus from the dead. They did not pretend that Lazarus

* John, xi. 4, 5.
† John, xi. 47.

was only apparently dead; they knew that, when he was raised to life, he had been buried for four days, and was in a state of decomposition. The power of Christ was so universally known, that the Jewish historian, Josephus, does not hesitate to call Him "a man mighty in working miracles."

4. The PROPHECIES of Christ are as well authenticated as His miracles. He foretold, among other things, the ruin of Jerusalem, the propagation of the Gospel, and the perpetuity of the Church which He founded.

5. DEATH OF CHRIST.—Christ laid down His life in testimony of His Divine Mission: He had proclaimed Himself the Son of God, and sealed His words with His blood on Golgotha. Caiphas the high-priest said to Him, "I adjure Thee by the living God, that thou tell us if Thou be Christ the Son of God. Jesus saith to him, I am. Nevertheless, I say to you, Hereafter you shall see the Son of man sitting on the right hand of the power of God, and coming in the clouds of heaven. Then the high-priest rent his garments, saying: He hath blasphemed: what further need have we of vitnesses? Behold now you have heard the

blasphemy: what think you? But they answering, said: He is guilty of death."* He was accused before Pilate of having called Himself the Son of God: "We have a law, and according to the law He ought to die; because He made Himself the Son of God."† It was the strict and solemn duty of Christ, if He had been misunderstood, to explain His meaning. He was adjured to do so in the name of the living God; He owed it to truth and Religion, for, if He was not God, He became the cause of idolatry to all His followers. Instead of giving any explanation, He repeated what He had said, and enforced it by referring to the last judgment and announcing that He himself would appear in the heavens to judge the world. It was universally known that He claimed to be the Son of God; while He was hanging on the Cross, the people said in derision, "If thou be the Son of God, come down from the Cross."‡ The centurion and his soldiers who were on guard near the Cross, when they saw the sun darkened, and felt the earth shaking under their feet, cried out in terror, "Indeed this was the Son of God."§

* Matt., xxvi. 63-66; Mark, xiv. 62.
† Luke, xix. 7.
‡ Matt., xxvii. 54.
§ Matt., xxvii. 54.

6. THE RESURRECTION.—The Divinity of the Mission of Christ, was fully established by His Resurrection. That unheard of event was first announced at Jerusalem by the guard which had been placed around the sepulchre. When it was preached for the first time by St. Peter on Pentecost, several thousands at once became Christians, among whom, as the Acts testify, there were a large number of Jewish priests. In the ranks of the Jewish priests were found the bitterest enemies of Christ, and they would never have become His followers, had not the miracle of His Resurrection been proved beyond all reasonable doubt. The Resurrection was the great argument that converted the heathen world. Nothing except its unquestionable truth could have induced the Apostles to announce it, or the priests of the Jews to believe it, or the proud heathens of Greece and Rome to renounce the lax morality of idolatry for the severe laws of the Gospel. No candid man who examines without prejudice the evidences of Christ's Divine Mission, can doubt for a moment, that He really was what He claimed to be, the Son of God, and consequently that His doctrines are Divine.

SIXTH CONCLUSIVE ARGUMENT.

THE UNDENIABLE DISSIMILARITY OF THE CHURCH OF CHRIST TO ANY PURELY HUMAN INSTITUTION.

Whoever believes in Christ, must believe what His Church teaches. Every proof that establishes the Divinity of Christ, demonstrates the Divine truth of His Church.

That there is no similarity between the Church of Christ and any purely human institution that has ever existed or can exist, is evident from what I have said in this work on the marks of the Church. As it is unnecessary to repeat what has been sufficiently demonstrated, I shall direct your attention, in this place, to one point only, the foundation of the Church and the miraculous propagation of the Gospel.

Every man who knows what was the condition of the world at the time when the Apostles went forth on their mission, will admit that the propagation of the Gospel is of itself alone an evident proof of the divinity of the Church of Christ. The world, as St. Augustine argues, was converted to Christianity either by miracle or without miracle: if the world was converted by miracle, our faith is divine; if without miracle, then the conversion itself is the greatest miracle that was ever wrought. The reasoning of St. Augustine is unanswerable.

St. Justin, in his argument for the Christian Religion, drew the attention of his countrymen to the gigantic obstacles which the faith had to encounter. He argued that a Roman citizen, before becoming a Christian, had to make so many sacrifices that it was impossible for him to be converted except upon irresistible evidence. "Reflect," he says, "that we were not born Christians. We lived long enough among you; we attended with you the philosophical lectures of your academies. Before becoming Christians we examined the matter earnestly and thoroughly; nothing but the weight of undeniable, evident truth could have impelled us to do what we did in becoming Christians."

The same thing might be repeated to you at the present day by those who left your ranks to become Catholics. They might say, You knew us intimately, and you are our witnesses that without the most decisive evidence we should never have become Catholics. Let this be a warning to you not to pass lightly over the claims of the Catholic Church: before rejecting them, examine them in earnest.

The Divinity of the Church of Christ is undeniable, as I have proved when speaking of the marks of the Church. The only question that now remains to be settled is, Which is the Church of Jesus Christ.

SEVENTH CONCLUSIVE ARGUMENT.

THE UNDENIABLE AXIOM OF SAINT AMBROSE— "WHERE PETER IS, THERE IS THE CHURCH."

The irresistible force of this axiom has been proved in the second chapter of this work. As surely as Christ said to Peter, "Thou art Peter, and upon this rock I will build my Church; I will give to thee the keys of the Kingdom of Heaven; feed my lambs, feed my sheep:" as surely as Pius IX. is the lineal successor of St. Peter, so certain it is that no Church has any claim to the title of Catholic, except the Church which is in communion with the successors of Peter, the Roman Catholic

Church. I have proved above that any separation from her, any change in her doctrine, and any possibility of such a change, are all equally inadmissible, absurd, insulting to the Divine authority and truth of Christ.

You have to determine whether you will follow St. Peter and his successors, or such men as Simon Magus, Arius, Macedonius, Eutyches, Nestorius, Pelagius, and the rest of the founders of schism and inventors of heresy down to Saint-Simon and Joe Smith.

The seven points which I have thus briefly discussed, must necessarily lead every Infidel who is candid, and capable of reasoning logically, to acknowledge that man wants a Divinely revealed Religion and consequently faith ; that this Divinely revealed Religion is the only means by which he can reach his eternal destiny; that of all Religions and Churches which claim a supernatural or Divine origin, the only really Divine Religion, is the Roman Catholic Church. That Religion every man must admit, that Church every man must enter, if he wishes to save his soul. The proofs I have offered are obvious and irrefutable. You must either admit them, or fall into absurdities.

Have you ever seen the suspension bridge near the Niagara Falls? Which would you prefer, to cross the bridge and reach the opposite shore, or to throw yourselves headlong into the troubled waters of the foaming cataract? You would deem the man insane who should seriously ask you such a question. Now each of my arguments places you in a similar situation. Either you must follow the logical train of my reasoning, and pass on from argument to argument to the final conclusion, or you must cast yourselves into an abyss of self-contradiction and absurdity.

I have only a few remarks to add, in answer to some of the common objections of Infidels against Divine faith and against the authority of the Christian Revelation.

SECTION II.

OBJECTIONS ANSWERED.

The first objection of unbelievers, and one of the strongest obstacles to their admission of the claims of the Catholic Church, is the incomprehensibility of several articles of faith. The incomprehensibility of an article of faith, is no valid objection against it; on the contrary, precisely because we must expect a Divinely established Church to teach a faith Divinely revealed, we must be prepared for the announcement of mysteries, or articles of belief surpassing the limits of human understanding. If the faith of the Church were in every respect evident, it would be a strong presumption against her claims as a Church Divinely instituted; indeed, in that case, a supernatural

Revelation would be altogether unnecessary Mysteries in a Divinely revealed Religion, are in perfect harmony with its distinctive character and essential constitution. Mysteries give additional strength to the arguments which demonstrate the truth of the Catholic Church, for if those arguments were not absolutely convincing, men of intelligence could never have been induced to believe in revealed mysteries. Before such men as Justin, Augustine, and others of like talent and genius, would believe the mysteries of the Incarnation and Transubstantiation, the infallible authority of the Catholic Church must have been demonstrated to them so as to leave no room for doubt.

When once the Divine institution and the infallibility of the Church have been demonstrated, it is no longer reasonable to object to any article of faith on the ground of its incomprehensibility. Even in the natural order, when the proof is evident, the mere objection of incomprehensibility is not a sufficient ground for doubt. We meet with incomprehensible objects at every step in the sphere of purely natural truths and experimental facts. I make bold to assert that some of the mysteries of reason and experience are far more incompre hensible than the profoundest mysteries of Catholic faith. I will give one or two proofs of it, both in the order of reason and in that of experience. Take the mysteries of the Trinity and Transubstantiation, and compare each of them with a mystery in the intellectual or experimental order.

You say, Who can believe that in one God there are three persons? Observing that by the three persons we do not understand three individuals, but three distinct relations subsisting in one nature, I ask you in my turn, Is this mystery more incomprehensible than the eternity of God? Reason can prove that there is a God, and that He exists without any beginning; but I ask you, Do you find it easier to conceive the mystery of existence without beginning, than the mystery of three persons in one God, as taught by the Catholic Church? The former is as obscure as the latter; or rather, if you look into treatises of Catholic theology, I am confident you will find it easier to form some idea of the Trinity than of God's eternal existence and His relation to time.

Reason, when placed between the alternative of incomprehensibility and self-contradiction, prefers the former to the latter, and rather chooses to believe what it cannot comprehend, than to deny it when the denial involves an absurdity. This is applicable to the mysteries of our Religion. We accept the incomprehensible, rather than deny the irresistible proofs of the infallibility of the Church, and by denying them contradict our reason. There are incomprehensibilities in our faith, but no contradictions. When the infallibility of the Church is proved, nothing more is needed. God is the author both of reason and Revelation; there are obscurities and mysteries in both.

This is further confirmed by the consideration of the other mystery, to which I have called your attention, viz., Transubstantiation.

In regard to Transubstantiation you ask, How is it possible that bread and wine can be changed into the Body and Blood of Christ? I ask you in my turn, Is the mystery of Transubstantiation, effected as it is by the immediate influence of God's infinite power, more inexplicable than the changes of substance, the transmutations, that you meet with in nature at every step? Can you explain the process of germination, growth, fructification? Can you tell how the same juices of the earth are changed into a boundless variety of plants and trees, and the juices of plant and tree into another endless variety of fruits. What secret power is it that causes one tree to produce oranges, another figs? How does the flower weave the same earthy substances into all the varieties of exuberant or delicate textures of vegetation? You do not question the powers which God has imparted to inanimate nature, yet are not these changes of substance, where only a mediate influence of Divine power takes place, a thousand times more incomprehensible than that Transubstantiation which is effected by a direct and immediate act of God's omnipotence? Is it not infinitely more incomprehensible that God should have been able to bestow on senseless objects so great a diversity of powers, than that by His own immediate act He should be able to effect the mystery of Eucharistic Transubstantiation?

Animal life is as full of mystery as the vegetable kingdom, and leads to the same conclusion. You wonder how bread and wine can be changed by the immediate act of Divine omnipotence, and you do not reflect that in your own body a more astonishing change of substance daily takes place. You eat bread and drink wine; the bread and wine are changed into the substance of your flesh and blood. Eucharistic Transubstantiation is less astonishing than this change of substance effected by the powers of nature under the mediate influence only of Divine power.

The process of vegetation and animal life may be regarded as a faint reflex in the natural order of an infinitely higher type of Transubstantiation in the Holy Eucharist; only the natural changes of substance, being more complicated, are less intelligible than the simple change produced by direct Divine intervention in the Eucharist. There is a real connection between natural and supernatural truth, and between all truths, because God, in whom all truth has its origin, is essentially one. Revelation being the work of God as well as the visible world, is very intimately connected with nature. I have always observed this mutual relation with the greatest satisfaction.

The intimate connection of reason and revealed Religion, is evident, also, when we compare the principles of philosophy with those of theology, as every professor of theology has occasion to observe, especially when after having taught theology, he returns, as I did, to the teaching of philosophy

EVERLASTING PUNISHMENT.

There is an article of faith which Infidel generally reject with the utmost scorn, an which by itself alone appears to them to be a sufficient reason to reject the whole of Christianity. That article is the Eternity of the Pains of Hell. Let us briefly examine what right they have to deny it.

The principal reason usually alleged against it, is the Infinite Mercy of God. Infidels pretend that Divine Mercy is in direct contradiction to Everlasting Punishment. But I ask, Why do not Infidels remember God's Infinite Justice, rather than His Infinite Mercy, when there is question of Divine punishment? Why do they not infer from the nature of Infinite Justice, that the punishment of grievous sin must be eternal, since the offense involves a real contempt of Infinite Majesty? Certainly, God is infinitely good, but He is, likewise, infinitely just. Because He is infinitely good, He rewards virtue with eternal beatitude. No one thinks of complaining of this, though an eternal reward, such as the beatific, everlasting vision of God, infinitely surpasses all purely human merits. Sovereign Justice requires that the punishment should bear an adequate proportion to the offense, and as man is incapable of undergoing torments which are infinite in intensity, it is but just that he should be subjected to punishments that are infinite in duration.

The eternity of Hell is a fearful truth, no doubt, and Infidels do their utmost to cast a doubt upon it, in order to stifle remorse, if possible, and to live on in sin with greater freedom. But their efforts are vain; they can never disprove, nor even render doubtful, the existence of Eternal Punishments. To deny them, is to act in direct opposition to reason. I shall prove it.

I grant that Eternal Punishments, are, in some respects, a mystery; but, I need only remind you, mysteries meet us on every side, when we attempt to investigate the relations that exist between the Creator and His works. This fact will not be disputed. Every man knows too well that he cannot comprehend the relation of God's eternity to time, nor of His Immutability to His Creative Act. There are mysteries, there must be mysteries, in the mutual bearings which exist between the Divin attributes and the physical and moral order of things. The finite cannot comprehend the Infinite; therefore it is wisdom to accept the clear teachings of Revelation on this as on all other subjects.

You cannot reject, as a falsehood, that upon which you cannot pronounce a final judgment: To do so, at the risk of eternal misery, this, assuredly, is a mode of acting which you yourselves, upon reflection, will pronounce in the highest degree unworthy of a reasonable being.

The audacity of Infidels in denying the Eternity of Hell, appears in a still more striking light, if we direct our attention to the numbers and authority of those who are arrayed against them. As compared with Infidels, believers in Everlasting Punishments, possess an immense preponderance of learning, talents, genius, as well as an incalculable majority of numbers. Infidels have against them the united testimony of all Christian nations, Catholic and non-Catholic, that have existed for eighteen hundred years. You know as well as we do, what a vast weight of genius, science, virtue is found in this immense multitude. Indeed, Infidels put themselves in opposition to the whole of mankind, for the Eternity of Hell has been the uniform belief of men in all ages. The civilized, the barbarian, and the savage, Jews, Mahommedans, pagans, all tribes and tongues, of which there exists any record, have agreed in that belief, dreadful and mysterious as it is. Take, among ancient nations, the highly cultivated Greeks and Romans: all who are acquainted with their literature, know that their philosophers, orators, and poets, speak of Everlasting Punishments in another life as of a doctrine universally prevalent. Thus Virgil sings,

> "Sedet, æternumque sedebit
> Infelix Theseus."*
> "Chained, *forever* chained, there pines
> Unhappy Theseus."

A large number of similar passages might be cited from Virgil, Ovid, Statius, and other ancient Latin poets. A great portion of the sixth book of the Æneid, and the eleventh of Homer's Odyssey, is a description of the torments of the wicked in Hades or Tartarus. The idea of the Furies, the Titans, of the wheel of Ixion, the stone of Sisyphus, the pool of Tantalus, is but the poetic embodiment of a

* Æn. l. VI. v. 617, 6.8.

universal conviction. Even Lucretius, a disciple of Epicurus, joins his testimony to that of all his cotemporaries:

" Ignis ubi ardebit nullo delebilis ævo."*
" Where fires shall glow, that Time shall never quench."

Plato, in his Gorgias, speaks of two kinds of punishments, one of which is inflicted for offenses that can be expiated, and the other for crimes that admit of no expiation : those who are guilty of this latter class of crimes, will, he says, be punished by "frightful torments forever."† I might offer endless quotations from writers of all ages and nations, with whose literature we are acquainted, or from the works of travelers in all regions of the globe. This universal belief must have a common origin, and no other origin can be assigned for it than reason itself enlightened by the universal tradition of a primitive Revelation.

Were the universal testimony of mankind in their favor, Infidels would be the first to appeal to it, but as it is against them, they are in the habit of passing it by in silence, and appealing exclusively to reason.

* Lucret. De Nat. Rerum.
† Plato, Dial. Gorgias.

But reason bears out the belief of mankind, and shows it to have its foundation in the very nature of sin and the Divine attributes. Though reason cannot fathom what is mysterious in Eternal Punishments, yet it can demonstrate that they are perfectly in accordance with the intimate nature of sin and the perfections of God.

In the first place, the malice of mortal sin is in its nature infinite, because, as I have observed, mortal sin involves a real contempt of Infinite Majesty.

In the next place, man is created for God alone. If he serves Him on earth, his bliss in the next world will be perfect: it is but just, if he deliberately refuses to serve Him, and contemns His law, that his misery in the next life should be complete. Man's happiness, to be perfect, must be eternal: his misery, to be complete, must be everlasting.

St. Gregory the Great assigns a third reason. "It is right," he says, " that they should never be freed from punishment, whose souls n this life were never free from sin, and that the punishment of a reprobate should never have an end, because while living he placed no bounds to his malice."* The Eye of God reads the secrets of all hearts : He would cease to be

† Greg. Magn. l. 34. Mor. c. 19.

God, were He incapable of inflicting a punishment proportioned to human depravity.

A fourth reason intimately connected with the receding, is the necessity of an adequate anction of the Divine law; that is, the law of God must be so enforced that, under all circumstances, there shall exist a motive powerful enough to deter men from transgressing it. This is due to the supreme and sacred character of the Divine law; but this demands that the punishment should be everlasting. Even in spite of Eternal Torments, men commit sin: what would happen, were they sure that Hell is not Eternal, and that all at last will be happy? The penalty would be clearly insufficient to enforce the law, and, for an immortal being, it would become contemptible. Human laws themselves, when properly enforced, have an adequate punishment attached to their transgression. You ask, Why does not God annihilate the sinner? Annihilation is an act of Divine omnipotence, rather than of justice. No one will call suicide an act of justice, yet it is an attempt at self-annihilation. Annihilation, so far from being an adequate sanction of the law of God, would serve to encourage vice, not to restrain it. If he is to be annihilated, the sinner might say with a triumphant contempt of God's Sovereign Justice, I will sin as much as I like; I care not for annihilation.

Everlasting Punishments, however fearful, are nothing more than an adequate sanction ot the law of God, or a vindication of the immutable sanctity of the moral order. To vindicate eternal order, is clearly an object of infinitely higher moment, than the endless misery resulting from wilful transgression. If, as you would fain believe, God cannot enforce His law by the infliction of Everlasting Punishment, immortal beings might insult him fearlessly: an immortal being might disregard any punishment that will at last terminate; and God would be no better than a feeble parent, who cannot or dares not curb and chastise the insolence of his offspring. But under the infliction of Eternal Torments even Satan trembles.

A fifth reason is founded on the very idea of human liberty and the probationary state of man on earth. It is in the highest degree worthy of Divine Wisdom, to have appointed for His creatures a period of probation, during which they may freely make their choice between good nd evil. That period of probation, as Revelation teaches, is limited to this life. It is in the very nature of a probationary state, that the final choice made during it, should be irrevocable. He who enters eternity guilty of mortal sin, places himself, of his own accord in a condition in which the guilt of mortal sin can no longer be expiated, because the period of probation and of grace is passed. The final choice, therefore, is in its own nature perpetual. In eternity, good and evil, light and darkness, are separated for evermore.

In this unalterable order of Providence, reason can discover no absurdity, but is forced to own its entire consistency with perfect Wisdom and Justice. Indeed, the most depraved scoffers at Religion, are so deeply convinced of the fitness of Eternal Punishments, that they cannot help secretly fearing their reality. Hence frequently their anger when Hell is spoken of in the pulpit. Were they convinced that an Everlasting Hell is a fable, they would laugh at our threats. The utmost an Infidel can say, is, that he doubts. If so, it is the part of a wise man to investigate; and if he discovers that Everlasting Punishments are a reality, reason commands him so to live as never to merit them. But to be in doubt, and yet to live as if the doubt were without foundation, or too unimportant to deserve attention, this is evidently to set reason at defiance. He who thus with unbounded recklessness exposes himself to eternal perdition, would deserve, indeed, that, if there was no Hell, God should create one for him especially, to punish so enormous an abuse of reason, so daring a defiance of God's Infinite Justice.

This reminds me of the well-known dialogue between a Christian and an Atheist. "What a fool you are," said the Atheist, "to be so anxious to avoid sin, if there is no hell." "And what a fool you are," replied the Christian, "for if there is a hell, you are sure to go there."

On this, as on so many other points, there is a glaring contradiction between the theory and the practice of Infidels. They admit that it is necessary to condemn certain criminals to perpetual imprisonment or even to death: but what is imprisonment for life, in the sphere of human justice, but a sort of Everlasting Punishment? Human laws, in your opinion, require it. Far weightier reasons, as I have just shown, require the infliction of Eternal Punishments for the vindication of the Divine Law.

Eternal exclusion from the happiness of heaven, cannot, by itself alone, be considered an adequate sanction of the Divine law. To a vast majority of men, the prospect of an eternal existence exempt from suffering, would appear a sufficient degree of bliss. In consideration of such an existence, a rebel spirit might despise the most enormous guilt. Nothing short of Everlasting Punishment, without a shadow of comfort, or hope of relief, can serve as an adequate *menace* to restrain men from the commission of crime. A man may have no love of God, nor desire for the happiness of heaven; his passions may be fierce, his pride satanic; still, if he makes *any right use* of his reason, Everlasting Punishments must appear to him a sufficient motive to deter him from violating the law of God.

The threat of Eternal Misery is necessary, especially, for beings whose destiny is supernatural. The mere exclusion from a supernatural beatitude, such as the Beatific Vision of God, would not possess the least efficacy as a means of checking the vicious. " The sensual man perceiveth not the things that are of the

Spirit of God : for it is foolishness to him, and he cannot understand "* Supernatural bliss awakens no desire in the hearts of sensual men: it inspires many of them with disgust.

But the bare thought of Everlasting Misery terrifies the most obdurate wretch. He cannot despise it. Rather than admit that vice will lead to Eternal Punishments, he questions their existence, and vainly labors to persuade himself that they are a fiction, and man's immortality itself a mere dream ; or he rushes headlong into the wild tumult of worldly pleasures, in order to forget the dreadful future. His language to-day is what the Book of Wisdom, thousands of years ago, represented as the vain reasonings of the wicked. " Our time is as the passing of a shadow. Come therefore, and let us speedily use the creatures as in youth. Let us fill ourselves with costly wine and ointments, and let not the flower of the time pass by us. Let us crown ourselves with roses, before they be withered: let no meadow escape our riot. Let none of us go without his part in luxury ; let us everywhere leave tokens of joy, for this is our portion, and this our lot. These things they thought, and were deceived, for their malice blinded them, and they knew not the secrets of God."†

* 1 Cor., ii. 14.   † Wisdom, ii.

Lastly, the two-fold sanction of the Divine law, is founded on the very nature of the Divine attributes. I have remarked above, that because God is infinitely good, He rewards the just with everlasting beatitude, and because He is infinitely just, He punishes the wicked with Everlasting Misery. I might have said, that it is the same infinite retributive Justice that rewards the virtuous and punishes the depraved forever. All the attributes of God are the same Divine nature—they are God Himself, and derive their various names only from their varied relations to creatures. The eternal Divine law itself, in the last analysis, is God. Eternal rewards and Everlasting Punishments are founded on the same retributive Justice identified in God with the eternal law: they are the two-fold mirror of the same Divine attribute.

The preceding remarks give me the right, I think, to draw the following conclusions: first, so far as Eternal Punishments are a mystery, reason has no right to pronounce a final judgment upon them; secondly, though we cannot fully comprehend the Eternity of Hell, nor pronounce a final judgment upon it, yet we can prove, by the mere light of reason, that it is in harmony with the Infinite Justice and

Wisdom of God; thirdly, as there is question here, besides, of a point of revealed doctrine. man must submit his judgment to the evident authority of Divine Revelation.

A time shall come when Christ Himself shall fulfil that solemn and most definite prediction, by which He wished to impress upon the minds of men the absolute necessity of submitting to His teachings. That day shall come when Christ shall say to the just, "Come, ye blessed of my Father," and to the wicked, "Depart, from me, ye cursed;" " and these shall go into everlasting punishment; but the just into life everlasting."*

I have proved the Divine mission of Christ; I have a right to say with St. Augustine, "He that is not roused by these words of thunder, is not merely asleep but dead."

As I have on all occasions spoken plainly throughout these pages, you must pardon me if I tell you, in conclusion, that the true reason why Infidels object to the doctrine of Eternal Punishments, is not that such punishments are absurd and impossible, but that, if the Eternity of Hell is a reality, they have but too much reason to dread it.

* Matt., xxv. 34, 41, 46.

PRETENDED CONTRADICTION OF REVELATION WITH GEOLOGY AND HISTORY.

After having thus answered the objections drawn from the mysteries, I will now briefly answer the objections drawn from geology and history.

Infidels object that the Catholic Church, founding her ideas on the Bible, teaches that the world is only about six thousand years old, whereas it is proved by undeniable geological observations that our globe has existed for many millions of years. Similar objections are made on historical grounds, and it is contended that human history can be traced back through a series of ages far exceeding the Christian computation.

In regard to the geological objection, I answer, in the first place, that the Church has never defined the duration of the period of time which elapsed between the creation of the first elements of the world, and their co-ordination on earth and in the heavens; in other words, between the epoch indicated by the first verse of Genesis, " In the beginning God created heaven and earth," and the other epoch when God said, "Let there be light."

Secondly, the Church has never defined that the days of the Mosaic cosmogony were days of twenty-four hours. This observation is a complete answer to every geological objection that can be brought against Divine Revelation.

Lastly, even taking the days of the Creation to be days of twenty-four hours, the geological objection has no force, for there is a most important distinction to be made, which usually is entirely overlooked, between the period of creation and the time subsequent to it. There is an immense difference between the activity of natural powers under the immediate influence of the creative act of God, at the moment of their creation, and their subsequent activity when they are permitted to act in accordance with the permanent laws of nature which God has given them. Many of you know that the progress of science often enables us to do in a few moments, what used to be, under other circumstances, the work of considerable time. The powers of nature during the creative epoch may have been able to effect in a short time what now requires thousands of years to be accomplished. God may have given to the world the appearance which it presents, in order to try our faith, our submission to revealed Religion.

The objections drawn from history have no force whatever. No doubt there have existed nations whose vanity has prompted them to claim an imaginary duration embracing countless centuries; but have they ever proved their claims by any historical document? They give us fables, and a confused mass of assertions; they have not even forged a history; they do not relate a single fact. No history of any nation reaches back to the time of Noe. It is, indeed, hard to conceive how the fabulous pretensions of national vanity, ever came to be brought forward as an objection against biblical history. Such tales may be good enough for the nursery; they are certainly unworthy of serious discussion.

The same must be said of the class of objections founded on the Sanscrit books and language, and on certain Egyptian monuments and hieroglyphic inscriptions. Some of those objections are in reality founded on nothing better than astrological conjectures; others on various kinds of inventions equally arbitrary; all of them are alike destitute of force and pertinence. They may agree with the prejudices of Infidels, but they are of no value in a serious and candid discussion. You cannot cite a single one which is worthy the serious notice of an intelligent man.

I return to the proposition that a logical mind must either admit the conclusiveness of the seven arguments which I have adduced, and their irresistible consequences, or remain convicted of self-contradiction and absurdity.

Yes, it is absurd, while you contemplate the universe, to say, There is no God.

It is absurd, while you look upon yourself as a reasonable being, to deny the immortality of the soul.

It is absurd, while you confess that there is a God, and that you are a reasonable and immortal being, to maintain that you have no essential relations to Him, that you have no truths to believe, no duties to fulfil, or, in other words, that there is no Religion.

It is absurd, while you grant that your reason is insufficient to guide you to salvation, to deny the necessity of Revelation.

It is absurd, while you proclaim Christ to have been the wisest and most virtuous of men, to maintain that He falsely pretended to be the Son of God.

It is absurd to pretend that the Church founded by Him, and endowed with all the marks of a Divine origin, has erred, or can err.

It is absurd, while you acknowledge that this Church was committed to the guidance of St. Peter and his successors, to deny that the Catholic Church, which is the only Church governed by the successors of St. Peter, is the true Church of Christ, and that out of her pale there is no salvation.

I know that if a man is determined to impugn the truth at all hazards, it is always in his power to urge sophistical objections, and by unreasonable cavils to hide its light from his own mind. If in the face of heaven and earth, in spite of the myriads of contingent beings of which the universe is composed, there are men who have the audacity to deny the existence of the Creator, and pretend to consider the world as the work of chance, it is no wonder that men are to be met with who, in the face of all arguments, will continue to deny the claims of the Catholic Church, and the divinity of Christ. But as St. Paul declares atheists inexcusable, because the existence of God is evident from the existence of the universe; so whoever refuses to recognize the Catholic Church as the Church of God, is inexcusably guilty, because the evidences of her claims are

so obvious and overwhelming, that no one who
examines them fairly can fail to be convinced.

I may compare the seven conclusive arguments which I have urged, to the seven thunders spoken of in the Apocalypse. Rolling on through the course of all centuries, they announce to Infidels and unbelievers the approach of the last awful judgment, when it shall be made clear before the world, that whoever has erred and perished, has erred and perished freely; when, as is affirmed in Holy Writ, the wicked will exclaim, "repenting and groaning for anguish of spirit," " We fools. . . . Therefore we have erred from the way of truth; and the light of justice hath not shined unto us; and the sun of understanding hath not risen upon us. . . . What hath pride profited us; or what advantages hath the boasting of riches brought us? All those things are passed away like a shadow." Notice these lamentations. Is it not pride that makes Infidels and unbelievers despise Catholics for their submission to the Church in matters of faith, or, as is often also the case, especially in this country, for their poverty? All this will be changed on the last day: " We fools esteemed their life madness and their end without honor. Behold now they are numbered among the children of God, and their lot is among the saints."

The utter impossibility of finding an excuse for their conduct, will crown the despair of unbelievers and infidels. Either they were convinced, and rejected the truth deliberately; or they wilfully refused to clear up their doubts, and discover the truth. Your error is wilful—this, like a flash of lightning that shatters while it illuminates, accompanies each of the seven arguments which I have placed before you. " Destruction is thy own," is the terrific inscription written on the portals of the eternal abyss, and the wail of self-reproach that forever re-echoes through all its fearful depths.

Here, dear friends and fellow-citizens, I conclude this appeal. You have no choice except THE CATHOLIC CHURCH—OR DESPAIR.

Every one who has read these pages without prejudice, must have understood clearly, that Protestantism, in its tendency, leads to Distress and Despair; that in its principle it involves absurdity; that in its prejudices it is founded on calumny; that in its last consequences it implies self-contradiction, and that in every point of view, it is a Religion at war with the human heart and intellect, and with human society.

The history of Protestantism confirms all I have advanced. Protestantism began by introducing division and discord among brethren; it has continued its work of division in its own bosom: religious animosity and hostile doctrines divide its sects; its work of division is forever progressing.

Luther, Calvin, and their adherents would have done well to amend their own lives; the faults which they had observed in individuals could not justify them in the rash and violent introduction of discord and hatred among millions of brethren.

The condition of the whole world would be far better than it is, if all Christian nations were still united in the same faith. No one can calculate the amount of misery and bloodshed that would have been avoided, if England, Germany, Sweden, Denmark, Prussia, and Russia had remained Catholic. If all these powers, instead of being actuated by religious jealousies, had united their efforts to convert idolatrous nations, particularly in Asia, there is but little doubt that, with the Divine assistance, they would have succeeded in that glorious undertaking.

A time will come when all our separated brethren will return to Catholic unity. "They shall be made one fold and one shepherd." Happy the time when the Christian world shall witness their return. The *Te Deum* which will then be intoned by the Sovereign Pontiff as Head of the Church, will be the most glorious and consoling ever intoned by the Vicar of Christ.

There is no country where a return to Catholic unity would bear richer fruits than in the United States; none where, even in a political and social point of view, it would be more desirable. *E pluribus unum*, is your national motto: nothing would contribute more effectually to keep the States united, than unity of faith. Sectarianism fosters animosity. Mutual charity and universal happiness would be greatly promoted, if, instead of the denominations which now divide the numerous families of all nations that have fixed their abode in this noble land, the spiritual authority of the only true Church of Christ were to unite them all in one communion of faith and hope.

May God in His infinite goodness hasten the time when this happy union of faith shall be accomplished in this glorious Republic. Let each one contribute his best efforts to bring about that auspicious event. This little work has been written for that purpose. I know that my arguments will not have the effect of making all my readers members of the Catholic Church and heirs of heaven; but I entertain the firm hope, and cherish the sweet consolation, that all who are sincere and resolute will be moved, by the perusal of this work, to inquire earnestly into the truth of the Catholic Religion, and I am sure that all who do so will, with the grace of God, become Catholics.

Nothing in the world could have induced me to leave my native country, but the desire which has prompted me to write these pages. My most earnest wish is to contribute, as far as I am able, to bring you to the knowledge of the truth, and place you in the path of salvation. Now that I have addressed you all, I shall leave this life with the sweet hope that I have fulfilled my duty towards you as my brethren in Jesus Christ, as my friends, and fellow-citizens.

If now and then I have made use of any harsh expressions, I hope you will forgive me, for the reason which I have alleged in the Preface. When speaking or writing on a subject of such vast importance as Religion, charity commands us to utter the truth frankly and fairly in the plainest language.

Once more I declare, in the presence of God, who searches the inmost recesses of the heart, that I have not the least bitterness of feeling against any religious denomination, but cherish in the depths of my soul the deepest affection for all. I am firmly persuaded that in all denominations of Christians, whether they are called Episcopalians, Presbyterians, Methodists, Baptists, or by whatever name they may be distinguished, there are noble-hearted men, who err not from malice, but because they have been born and brought up in Protestantism, and have never earnestly examined the religious questions discussed in these pages. Those sincere and candid men will read my arguments with the same pure intention, the same calm and earnestness, with which I have written them, and will, with the aid of Divine grace, derive from them the fruit of conversion which they are intended to produce.

I say *with the aid of Divine grace*, because faith, after all, is a gift of God. No arguments, however powerful, no evidence, however convincing, can impart Divine faith. Humility and prayer are necessary. It is necessary to say with the centurion of the Gospel, " I do believe, Lord ; help Thou my unbelief." Give me strength to proceed in my inquiries, to accomplish what Thy grace has shown me to be necessary for my salvation, and to be a member of Thy Church.

I know, said Du Perron, that I can convince any man of error, and prove to him the undeniable truth of the Catholic Church ; but I cannot convert heretics : for that purpose I send them to the Bishop of Geneva. He referred to St. Francis de Sales, at that time Bishop of Geneva, who had the gift of softening the hearts of men. It is not enough to convince the mind, the heart must be converted.

St. Paul could convince Agrippa, and terrify Felix ; but even St. Paul could not convert men who refused to be converted. When the will obstinately resists the grace of conversion, the most that can be obtained is a confession like that of Agrippa, " Thou almost persuadest me to be a Christian ;" or like that of the Areopagites, " We will hear thee again concerning this matter."

There are but too many who thus resist the grace of God. For such men all argument is in vain. Unless you humble yourselves before God, and have recourse to prayer, you will not be converted. You will say at best, Your arguments have almost made me a Catholic. I will again consider the subject at some future time.

Who has promised you that the time which you hope for, will be granted? "To-day, if you shall hear His voice, harden not your hearts." To-day, while you are reading these pages, you hear the voice of God; pray to God that you may clearly understand the truth, and resolve to embrace it.

Never will you find peace or hope, unless you obey your convictions. On the other hand, you will be sure to enjoy peace, if following the inspirations of grace and the dictates of your conscience, you ask with the sincerity of St. Paul, "Lord, what wilt Thou have me to do?" and if, without delay, with a mind fully made up, you follow the known will of God.

Many an Elymas will do his best to prevent you from becoming Catholics. You will have to encounter the reproaches of those whose interest it is to uphold Protestantism; you will have to meet and conquer the still more formidable influence of popular opinion. But why should we seek to please men rather than God? Why should a man be ashamed to avow his convictions, especially in this free country? Why should he lack the courage to do that on which all the consolations of his life and all his hopes for eternity depend? But one thing is necessary, and that is to render yourself pleasing to God by leading a life worthy of the Catholic faith. I have endeavored to contribute towards this object, by a work entitled "A Manual of the Catholic Religion for Self-Instruction."

On all subjects, except the Catholic Church, your national character is eminently distinguished by a spirit of inquiry. Look into our doctrines seriously, earnestly, impartially, as was recently done by one of your eminent men, Judge Burnett, formerly Governor of Oregon. Read his work, "The Path which led a Protestant Lawyer to the Catholic Church." Conducting his investigation upon principles similar to those which govern legal proceedings, he compared the Protestant with the Catholic doctrine, consulted eminent writers on both sides, and became a Catholic. Adopt this or any other method which you may prefer, but by all means, if you love the truth, and wish to be saved, examine the Catholic religion, and examine it with earnestness and impartiality, and you shall return to the bosom of the Mother Church, from which violence and calumny separated your ancestors, and from which the prejudices of birth and education have kept you alienated.

If any one of you, after having become a Catholic, should be asked the reason why he has taken such a step, let him answer with La Harpe, "Mes amis, j'ai examiné, et je crois; examinez, et vous croirez.—My friends, I have examined, and I believe; examine, and you will believe."

Earnest examination united with fervent prayer will surely lead you to the Catholic Church, the Mother of knowledge, of holy hope and holy love, the ever-flowing source of consolation in time, and the only guide to a blissful eternity, through Jesus Christ our Lord, her Founder. Amen.

THE END.

www.ingramcontent.com/pod-product-compliance
Lightning Source LLC
Chambersburg PA
CBHW020326240426
43673CB00039B/930